The World of
Van Gogh

TIME-LIFE LIBRARY OF ART

The World of Van Gogh

1853-1890

by Robert Wallace
and
the Editors of TIME-LIFE BOOKS

TIME-LIFE BOOKS, New York

TIME-LIFE BOOKS

FOUNDER: Henry R. Luce 1898-1967

Editor-in-Chief: Hedley Donovan
Chairman of the Board: Andrew Heiskell
President: James R. Shepley
Chairman, Executive Committee: James A. Linen
Group Vice President: Rhett Austell

Vice Chairman: Roy E. Larsen

MANAGING EDITOR: Jerry Korn
Assistant Managing Editors: David Maness,
Martin Mann, A. B. C. Whipple
Planning Director: Oliver E. Allen
Art Director: Sheldon Cotler
Chief of Research: Beatrice T. Dobie
Director of Photography: Melvin L. Scott
Senior Text Editor: Diana Hirsh
Assistant Art Director: Arnold C. Holeywell

PUBLISHER: Joan D. Manley
General Manager: John D. McSweeney
Business Manager: John Steven Maxwell
Sales Director: Carl G. Jaeger
Promotion Director: Paul R. Stewart
Public Relations Director: Nicholas Benton

TIME-LIFE LIBRARY OF ART
SERIES EDITOR: Robert Morton
Associate Editor: Diana Hirsh
Editorial Staff for *The World of Van Gogh:*
Picture Editor: Kathleen Shortall
Designer: Paul Jensen
Staff Writers: John von Hartz, Paula Pierce,
Lucille Schulberg, David Lawton
Chief Researcher: Martha T. Goolrick
Researchers: Lynda Kefauver, Gail Hansberry,
Suzanne Seixas
Art Assistant: Mervyn Clay

EDITORIAL PRODUCTION
Production Editor: Douglas B. Graham
Assistant: Gennaro C. Esposito
Quality Director: Robert L. Young
Assistant: James J. Cox
Copy Staff: Rosalind Stubenberg (chief), Patricia Miller,
Florence Keith
Picture Department: Dolores A. Littles, Catherine Ireys

About the Author

Robert Wallace has published more than 100 nonfiction articles as well as numerous short stories and poems. He is the author of *Rise of Russia* in TIME-LIFE BOOKS' Great Ages of Man series, *The Grand Canyon* and *Hawaii* in the American Wilderness series, and three other Library of Art volumes, *The World of Leonardo*, *The World of Rembrandt* and *The World of Bernini*. The present book and its predecessors are the fruit of more than four years' study in European and American museums and libraries.

The Consulting Editor

H. W. Janson is Professor of Fine Arts at New York University, where he is also Chairman of the Department of Fine Arts at Washington Square College. Among his numerous publications are *The Sculpture of Donatello* and *History of Art*.

The Consultant for This Book

Seymour Slive is Professor of Fine Arts and Chairman of the Department of Fine Arts at Harvard University. He has also taught at Oberlin College and Pomona College and has been an exchange professor at the University of Leningrad. Dr. Slive, the recipient of a Guggenheim Fellowship, was honored by the Dutch government as an Officer of the Order of the House of Orange-Nassau for his work on a Frans Hals exhibition in Haarlem. He is the author of numerous books and articles on Dutch painting.

On the Slipcase

During his stay in the southern French town of Arles, Van Gogh traveled 25 miles farther south to see the Mediterranean at a village called Saintes-Maries-de-la-Mer. He wrote to his brother Theo that the sea "has the colors of mackerel. . . . You don't know if it is green or violet, you can't even say it's blue, because the next moment the changing light has taken on a tinge of pink or gray." And he wrote to a friend: "On the beach, quite flat and sandy, there are little boats, green, red and blue, so pretty in form and color that one is reminded of flowers." The full painting from which the detail on the slipcase is taken appears on page 185; a sketch of the scene is on page 154.

End Papers

Front and Back: These two drawings of orchards in Provence were made by Van Gogh within a year of each other—between April 1888 and the spring of 1889—and show a marked change in his style. The dots and lines of the early sketch *(front)* are transformed into swirls in the latter. Some experts connect this change with Van Gogh's increasingly disturbed mental state, but more likely it was an evolution of his graphic technique.

The following individuals and departments of Time Inc. helped to produce this book: Editorial Production, Norman Airey; Library, Benjamin Lightman; Picture Collection, Doris O'Neil; Photographic Laboratory, George Karas; TIME-LIFE News Service, Murray J. Gart; Correspondents Maria Vincenza Aloisi (Paris), Letje H. C. Endt-Van der Horst (Amsterdam), Margot Hapgood (London), Elisabeth Kraemer (Bonn) and Ann Natanson (Rome).

Contents

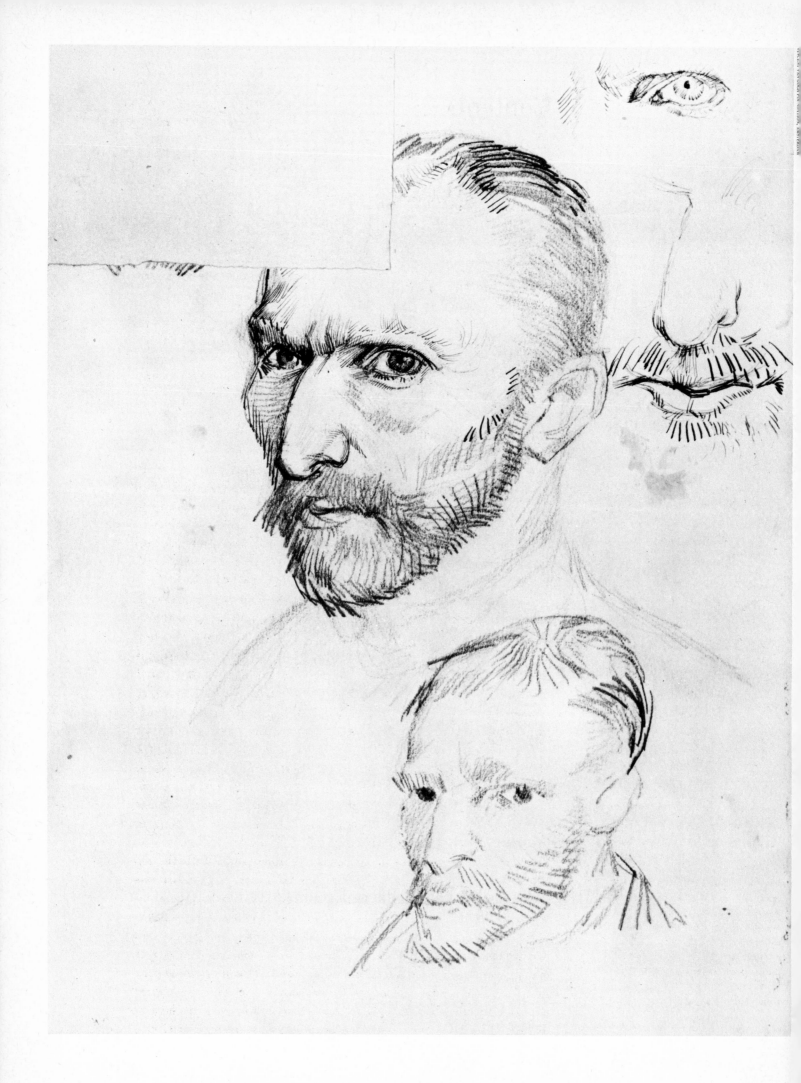

6

I

The
Misfit

If there is one fact about Vincent van Gogh that is well known, it is that he cut off his ear and gave it to a prostitute. The act is not at all important in itself, but it is wildly disconcerting, and obscures the whole picture of the artist. Even the most sophisticated reader, on picking up a book about Van Gogh, cannot help but wonder when he will come to the part about the ear. In anticipating it, he may skim over information that is a hundredfold more pertinent. Having got past it, he may feel that all else is anticlimactic. Perhaps it is best to meet the problem head-on: the part about the ear will be found at the end of Chapter 5.

Now that the ear (in fact merely the ear lobe) has been removed, it may be possible to take a more relaxed view of the unhappy man who removed it. Vincent van Gogh, who died at 37, in 1890, had one of the briefest careers in art history. It spanned only 10 years—and of these, the first four were devoted almost exclusively to drawing. But the volume of his output was astonishing. Close to 1,700 of his works survive, almost 900 drawings and more than 800 paintings, made in volcanic outbursts of creation that sometimes saw him produce a canvas a day for weeks on end. During his lifetime he sold only one painting (for the equivalent of $80), and among his last recorded words was the question, "But what's the use?" The use, of course, became apparent within 25 years after his death. Together with Paul Cézanne, Georges Seurat and Paul Gauguin, Van Gogh is now ranked as one of the founding fathers of modern art.

Van Gogh's work is of an extremely personal sort. With the exception of his countryman Rembrandt, no other great artist has produced more self-portraits (more than 40). His landscapes, figures, interiors and still lifes are in a sense self-portraits as well. It was his method to fuse what he saw, and what he felt, as quickly as possible into statements that were revelations of himself. His color and his warmth are so powerful that looking at one of his paintings can be like staring into the blue, yellow and orange flames beyond the suddenly opened door of a furnace. It is not that he had an apocalyptic vision of the fires of hell. On the contrary, few men have ever had greater capacity to give love, or greater need to receive it. Sadly, he could express his love only in his art. When he sought to express it directly to other human beings he met only misunderstanding or hostility. "One may have a blazing hearth in one's soul," he wrote, "and yet no one ever comes to sit by it. Passersby see only a wisp of smoke rising from the chimney and continue on their way."

While he was alive Van Gogh was regarded as an exceedingly difficult, obstinate and even frightening man. Now that he has been safely in his grave for fourscore years, he is widely viewed as a hero. To an age that seems dedicated to the obliteration of the individual, he stands out as an early anti-establishment resistance fighter of the first rank. It is true that he took his own life, but not until he had fought harder, against greater odds, than a man can reasonably be expected to do. He saw the world as an intolerable botch, something God had put together "in a hurry on one of His bad days," and he took the only honorable course: a doomed struggle. Moreover, he did not consider himself a hero, which makes his bravery even more authentic. "It is very probable that I shall have to suffer a great deal yet," he wrote, "and to tell the honest truth, under no circumstances do I long for a martyr's career. For I have always sought something different from heroism, which I do not have, which I certainly admire in others, but which, I tell you again, I consider neither my duty nor my ideal."

Vincent's mother, Anna Carbentus van Gogh, is revealed in the photograph above and in her son's affectionate portrait below as a lively woman with a sense of humor. Having lost a child before Vincent, she was especially protective of him as a boy. She once became furious when her mother-in-law boxed little Vincent's ears for some minor offense. It took Pastor van Gogh a full day to make peace between the two women in his home.

He was often inclined to belittle himself in other ways. He signed his works—when indeed he did sign them—not "Vincent van Gogh" or "Van Gogh" but merely "Vincent." He once attempted to pass this off by saying that in France, where his greatest paintings were produced, his last name was unpronounceable. But in fact, his earlier paintings, made in Holland, also bear only the name "Vincent." It is as though he was always sending urgent, affectionate messages to someone, anyone, who might be kind enough to accept him as a friend.

His Christian names were Vincent Willem, after his grandfathers, and the "Gogh" probably derived from a small town on the Dutch-German border. Among his ancestors were various preachers, state executives, consuls, goldsmiths and a successful sculptor—a solid lot. He was born on March 30, 1853, in the village of Groot Zundert in the Dutch province of North Brabant near the southern (Belgian) frontier. His father, Theodorus, was pastor of a small Dutch Reformed church. Theodorus was called "the handsome dominie" and was beloved by his parishioners, but he was not overly gifted with intelligence or eloquence —all the "promotions" in his career were lateral, from one obscure village to another. Vincent's mother, Anna Cornelia Carbentus, was a similarly mild and uninspired soul. It is common for biographers to dismiss Van Gogh's parents with a wave of the hand—and perhaps that judgment is correct. Their bourgeois outlook on life, with its narrow-minded emphasis on proprieties and outward appearances, was the opposite of his own. But it is only fair to say that the parents were very decent people in their fashion; if they had difficulty understanding their remarkable son, so did many others.

It is an equally presumptuous business to indulge in posthumous psy-

choanalysis of Van Gogh, although a number of accredited experts have tried it. One fact that has been noted is that although Vincent was the eldest of the Van Gogh children, he was not the first. One year before his birth, to the very day, his mother was delivered of another child, also a boy, and also named Vincent Willem van Gogh. He was stillborn. His grave was near the church door, which the second Vincent, with the identical name and the same birthday, walked past every Sunday of his childhood. This could not have been pleasant, and there is a flat statement in the Van Gogh family papers that the name of the dead predecessor was mentioned often in Vincent's presence. But whether that had any bearing on his "guilt feelings" or his supposed sense of being "an inadequate usurper" remains wide open to doubt.

There were several other children in the family of Pastor Theodorus, two boys and three girls, but of these only one was of great importance to Vincent: Theo, whose life was inextricably and tragically intertwined with that of his elder brother. Without the support and almost superhuman understanding of Theo, four years younger, Vincent's art —and indeed his life—would have come to nothing.

As to older relatives, Vincent was plentifully supplied with aunts and uncles, all of them exemplary citizens. Two of his aunts married military men who became generals. One of his uncles achieved the highest rank in the navy, vice-admiral, and served as commandant of the Amsterdam navy yard. No fewer than three other uncles were successful art dealers, and one of them, also named Vincent, accumulated a fortune. "Uncle Cent," as he was called, was a partner in the French firm of Goupil & Cie., which in addition to its headquarters in Paris had branches in The Hague, London, Brussels and Berlin. (The well-known New York art gallery, M. Knoedler & Co., was founded by the man who was Goupil's American agent.) Uncle Cent was not only rich; he was childless, and there was reason for the family to suppose that he would one day make young Vincent his heir.

Vincent's father, the Reverend Theodorus van Gogh, was a handsome man, as his photograph shows. But he was not an eloquent preacher, and spent his 36-year ministry in out-of-the-way villages. Vincent's drawing *(below)*, done in 1881, uncompromisingly shows the effects of age on his father. The relationship between father and son was not intimate. The stolid Dutch Reformed minister ran a disciplined household, and often disapproved of Vincent's renegade behavior.

As a boy Vincent displayed a good deal of charm. Red-haired, freckled, with pale blue eyes that sometimes deepened to green, he was fond of collecting beetles and vacant birds' nests, and had an amiable knack for inventing games. His younger brothers and sisters loved his company; after one particularly pleasant day, they formally made him a present of a rosebush that happened to be growing in their father's garden. But Vincent was also stubborn and hot-tempered, given to strangely contrary behavior. He once modeled a small elephant in clay and made a striking sketch of a cat, but when his parents praised them, he immediately destroyed them. It is likely that the praise embarrassed him.

At 12 he was sent to boarding school in the village of Zevenbergen, 15 miles away. His father could ill afford the expense but seems to have become convinced that his son was getting too "rough" through his association with the peasant boys of Groot Zundert. The separation from his family at such an age doubtless left its mark on Vincent. In later years he wrote touchingly of his joy at reunion with his father. Very little is known of his education at Zevenbergen, beyond the fact that he emerged from it with a vast appetite for reading. For the remainder of

Vincent's mother, Anna, expressed her love of nature in needlework and in drawings like the flower study below, which she did in 1844. Vincent's pencil drawing of a plant *(above)*, probably copied from a book, suggests his mother's influence. As a boy Vincent was not thought artistically gifted, but here he reveals fine draftsmanship for an 11-year-old.

his life he was fascinated by books. They appear, with legible titles, in many of his paintings, and he read them with what may at first seem to be a curious lack of discrimination. He admired Shakespeare, but also thought that *La Case de l'Oncle Tom (Uncle Tom's Cabin)* was a noble piece of literature. Keats, Voltaire, Homer, the French moralist Ernest Renan and the historian Jules Michelet had Vincent's utmost respect—but he rated their writings no more highly than he did Dickens' *Christmas Carol.* Vincent's taste in art was equally startling. He once said that he would give 10 years of his life for the privilege of being allowed to sit for two weeks with a loaf of bread in front of Rembrandt's magnificent *Jewish Bride,* but he also revered a number of long-forgotten hacks who made magazine illustrations. A common denominator can be found, however, in most of the writers and artists Vincent admired: they dealt with the destitute and downtrodden. It did not matter that the treatment was often oozily sentimental and patronizing; what moved him was the subject.

At 16 Vincent left school, probably because of financial pressure. Through the influence of Uncle Cent a place was found for him in the office of Goupil & Cie. at The Hague. Goupil's was a conservative house, specializing in well-made reproductions of famous paintings. (The Paris headquarters also dealt in contemporary originals, but only by noncontroversial artists.) At Goupil's he went to work with a will, displaying none of the "eccentricities" that would later make his life wretched. He enjoyed his job and was apparently successful at it. When Vincent had been in The Hague for about three years Theo came for a visit, and soon thereafter the two brothers—they were then 19 and 15—began to exchange letters.

Only 36 of Theo's letters have been preserved, but 661 of Vincent's were carefully kept by Theo. (Another 135, addressed to other members of the family and to friends, also exist.) The letters are so vivid in style and so revealing of Van Gogh's innermost feelings that they constitute a superb autobiography. The first few items in the correspondence are short and simple: Vincent dispenses brotherly advice, suggesting that Theo take up pipe smoking "as a remedy for the blues," and that he study the work of various writers and painters. In time, however, the letters become full of intimate explanations of Van Gogh's life and art. Many of them are thousands of words in length, and all together they span an 18-year period, beginning in August 1872 and ending in July 1890. The last letter to Theo, unfinished, was found in Van Gogh's pocket after he had shot himself.

When he was 20 Vincent was transferred, with a fine recommendation, to the London branch of Goupil's. He was sorry to leave Holland, but London, he wrote, would "be splendid for my English, [which] I can understand well enough, but . . . cannot speak as well as I should wish." He found a room in the home of a widowed Frenchwoman, Mrs. Loyer, who with her daughter Ursula kept a small day school for boys, and for a time his letters to Theo were full of cheer. He planted a flower garden for the Loyers, roamed happily through London, enjoyed boating on the Thames and went so far as to buy a top hat—"you cannot be in London without one." He also made a grievous miscalculation in regard to his landlady's daughter, Ursula, and thus began the first of his several disastrous encounters with women. He fell in love with the girl, but evidently did not bother to tell her. Throughout his life Van Gogh was given to weaving dreams in which he saw the world not as it was but as he wanted it to be; when he exposed his dreams he was devastated to find that no one shared them. In the case of Ursula he assumed that the girl returned his love, or, at the least, that she would return it as soon as he stated his feelings. When at last he did, after about a year, he discovered that the thought of loving him had never entered her head.

Although others may find something faintly comic in the picture of the childishly optimistic young Dutchman with his thick accent, his incongruous hat and his lack of perception of the girl's feelings, the blow to Vincent was terrific. In the wake of his rejection he moved to other quarters where he lived alone, rarely seeing anyone and writing seldom. When he did communicate, his letters contained enigmatic Biblical quotations and fragments of melancholy poetry copied from whatever book he happened to be reading. His parents became concerned about his health; one of his uncles visited London, and apparently returned with a gloomy report. The word "peculiar" began to be applied to him. In 1875 Uncle Cent arranged for him to be transferred to the Paris office in the hope that his spirits might be revived by a change in scene. As he departed London, well aware that his family and employers took a dim view of his behavior, Vincent closed a letter with a quotation from Ernest Renan that was to become his own credo: "Man is not on this earth merely to be happy, nor even to be simply honest. He is there to realize great things for humanity, to attain nobility and to surmount the vulgarity in which the existence of almost all individuals drags on."

This photograph shows Vincent at 13. He had the tousled hair, ruddy complexion and broad shoulders of a country youth, but these features were dominated by an arresting, melancholy gaze. Shy and withdrawn at boarding school, he was more playful during holidays at home, teasing his brothers and sisters and inventing games for them in the wheat fields and pine forests of Brabant. In four years at school, Vincent gave no inkling of later artistic genius, and made no lasting friends among his classmates.

In Paris Van Gogh's religious brooding increased. Theo, who by that time had also had the benefit of Uncle Cent's intercession and was employed by Goupil's in Brussels, was bombarded with more verses from the Bible and the full texts of hymns. Vincent roomed in Montmartre with a fellow-employee at Goupil's, a British youth named Harry Gladwell. Young Gladwell had religious leanings too, but seems to have been overwhelmed by Vincent, who was well on the way to becoming a fanatic. Of nights, Vincent read the Bible aloud ("We intend to read it all the way through"). He became increasingly careless in his work. He dissuaded customers from buying pictures of which he did not approve, and at the height of the Christmas buying season in 1875, he went off to Holland to visit his parents. When he returned he provoked his own dismissal by asking the manager a question that could be answered in only one way: were there any complaints against him? He was given three months' notice, perhaps in deference to his Uncle Cent's status, and thus six years of training as an art dealer came to an end. There was no visible regret on Vincent's part; he was not yet a rebel, but a dropout. To Theo he wrote only, "When the apple is ripe, a soft breeze makes it fall from the tree; such was the case here. . . ."

He was almost 23, unemployed, and had not the slightest idea what he would do next. Although he had frequently made sketches as accompanying illustrations to his letters, he seems not to have thought seriously of becoming an artist.

Still hoping perhaps that he might find some way of persuading Ursula Loyer to change her mind, Vincent decided to return to England. Through want ads in the British press he found a job as a teacher in a boarding school at Ramsgate. It was a place that Dickens might have relished. Vincent wrote of numerous insects, of dark stairways and passages, of "the room with the rotten floor" where the boys bathed at six washstands under the dim light from a "window with broken panes." Vincent was given room and board, but no salary, and worked hard. During the day he taught elementary French, German and arithmetic, and after school hours he kept an eye on the boys, "so that my time is pretty well taken up. . . ." It was an impossible situation and in a few months he altered it, though scarcely for the better as far as money was concerned. He took another teaching job at a school in Isleworth, near London, where the pay was very low but his duties were closer to his heart—he taught Bible classes and was occasionally allowed to preach at a local Methodist chapel. He sent Theo the text of one of his sermons. It speaks of the hardness of man's lot on earth, of the benevolence of God, and concludes that "we are all brothers."

In December 1876, after months of genteel semistarvation, Vincent went home for the holidays. His parents, who now lived in a small parish in Etten, were appalled by his distraught and emaciated appearance. It was decided that it would be pointless for him to return to England, and once again Uncle Cent was called upon. Uncle Cent, a hardheaded businessman, was disappointed in Vincent: "Supernatural things I may not know," said Uncle Cent, "but I know everything about natural things." Vincent, for his part, had some reservations about Uncle Cent and quoted the French writer Sainte-Beuve in regard to him: "In most men there exists a poet who died young, whom the man survived." Nevertheless, the uncle used his influence once again, this time to get Vincent a job as a clerk in a bookstore in Dordrecht. But his spirit was not in his employment; the job lasted less than four months.

Many years later the son of the bookstore manager offered some interesting recollections of Vincent as a bookseller's clerk. He recalled that Vincent spent his "working" hours surreptitiously translating the Bible into French, German and English, and that he also made sketches of which the bookseller did not approve—"silly pen-and-ink drawings, a little tree with a lot of branches and side branches and twigs." (Later, when Vincent became famous, the bookseller's son ransacked Vincent's old desk, hoping to find a few such silly sketches, but was not rewarded.) Another acquaintance from the Dordrecht days was a young schoolteacher, P. C. Görlitz, who shared a room with Vincent in a boardinghouse. Görlitz remembered that fellow boarders made fun of Vincent because "at table he said lengthy prayers and ate like a penitent friar: for instance, he would not take meat, gravy, etc. And then his face always had an abstracted expression—pondering, deeply serious, melancholy."

By the time his employment in the bookstore had been terminated, it was plain that Vincent's destiny was to become a clergyman—or so, at least, Vincent thought. His family questioned whether, at 24, he could apply himself to the rigorous studies that were required; nevertheless, they rallied around him. It was arranged that he study for the ministry in Amsterdam, and he went to live with his uncle Johannes, the admiral. The family engaged a tutor, Mendes da Costa, a fine scholar who was only a few years older than Vincent, and Vincent began lessons in Latin and Greek in order to prepare himself for theological-school examinations. The two young men got along well, although there was a certain incongruity in their relationship: Da Costa, readying his pupil for the Christian ministry, was a Jew.

Vincent studied diligently, but the effort was foredoomed. As Da Costa noted in a memoir of 1910, "After a short time the Greek verbs became too much for him. However I might set about it, whatever trick I might invent to enliven the lessons, it was no use. 'Mendes,' he would say . . . 'do you seriously believe that such horrors are indispensable to a man who wants to do what I want to do: give peace to poor creatures and reconcile them to their existence here on earth?' "

The tutor secretly agreed, but could not say so aloud. Vincent would try again, "but before long the trouble would start afresh, and then he would come to me in the morning with an announcement I knew so well, 'Mendes, last night I used the cudgel again,' or, 'Mendes, last night I got myself locked out again.' It should be observed," Da Costa continued, "that this was some sort of self-chastisement. . . . Whenever Vincent felt that his thoughts had strayed farther than they should have, he took a cudgel to bed with him and belabored his back with it; and whenever he was convinced that he had forfeited the privilege of spending the night in his bed, he slunk out of the house [and slept] on the floor of a little wooden shed, without bed or blanket. He preferred to do this in the winter. . . ."

After more than a year of study with Da Costa, Vincent gave up; he did not even attempt the examinations. It was not in Latin and Greek, he thought, that he would find the necessary knowledge to help him in comforting mankind, but "at the free course in the great university of misery." In August 1878—he was then 25 years old—he enrolled in a training school for lay preachers in Brussels. Graduates of the school were not full-fledged ministers, but received enough instruction to enable them to spread the Gospel and do missionary work among the poor. The school accepted Vincent on a probationary basis. He was given to understand that if he performed well he might be assigned a mission somewhere in Belgium. But he did not perform well. One of his fellow students recalled that during a grammar lesson, when Vincent was asked whether a word was nominative or dative, he replied, "Oh, sir, I really don't care." At the conclusion of the probationary period, no mission was offered to him. Instead, with such small support as his father could give, Van Gogh went unsponsored to the grim coal-mining region in southern Belgium called the Borinage, hoping that if his work was satisfactory, he might later receive a formal assignment from the school.

Van Gogh's letters from the Borinage are vividly descriptive. "Everywhere around one sees the big chimneys and the immense heaps of coal at the entrance to the mines. . . . Most of the miners are thin and pale from fever and look tired and emaciated, weatherbeaten and prematurely aged, the women as a whole faded and worn. Round the mine are poor miners' huts with a few smoke-blackened dead trees, thorn hedges, dunghills, ash heaps, slag. . . ."

He went deep underground, almost half a mile, to watch the miners working in little cubicles "like the cells in a beehive . . . or like the partitions in a crypt." He saw children loading coal on horse-drawn carts in the dim light of lamps "reflected as in a stalactite cave." He nursed the victims of explosions, cave-ins, fires and disease. He preached in an old dance hall, started a Bible school and—for a time—thought he had at last found the work for which he had been born. The missionary society in Brussels was impressed; he was given a six-month trial appointment as lay preacher at a salary of $10 a month.

But unfortunately, Vincent read his Bible with too literal an eye—in the opinion of the missionary society. He soon began to take the precepts of the New Testament as though they were Gospel. "Sell that thou hast, and give it to the poor" seemed to him a straightforward directive. Accordingly he moved out of his comfortable room in a baker's house and took up lodging in a wretched shack where he slept on the floor. He gave away the clothing with which his family had outfitted him, replacing it with a secondhand military tunic and a homemade sackcloth shirt. He let the coal dust remain on his face, lest he seem conspicuous among the begrimed miners. When he needed bandages for an injured man he tore up his own linen. His superiors reproached him for "excessive zeal," but he paid no heed. Finally, the missionary society dismissed him.

He remained in the Borinage, living on crusts. Apparently as the result of a family conference, Vincent's brother Theo was sent to reason with him. Theo, by this time, had done well in the firm of Goupil & Cie. and was a sound young man, the mainstay of his parents and the only Van Gogh to whom Vincent might listen. Theo had great affection for Vincent and recognized his potential—indeed, Theo had already suggested to Vincent that he become an artist. On this visit, however, Theo was obliged to carry out the family's wishes and present Vincent with various helpful ideas. Was Vincent not too fond of living in "idleness"? Might it not be well to consider a career as an engraver, perhaps, or a carpenter, bookkeeper or baker?

Vincent was hard-pressed to reply. "May I observe," he subsequently wrote Theo, "that this is a rather strange sort of 'idleness'? It is somewhat difficult for me to defend myself, but I should be very sorry if, sooner or later, you could not see it differently." Soon afterward Vincent submerged, withdrawing into an obscurity that has never been penetrated. He did not write to his brother for nine months, during which he seems to have passed through a fearsome mental and emotional crisis. He remained in the Borinage, but precisely how he managed to feed and clothe himself is not known. When at last he surfaced again, in a letter of four thousand words, he wrote Theo of his withdrawal in this analogy: "What molting time is to birds, so adversity or misfortune is . . . for us human beings. One can stay in it . . . one can also emerge renewed, but it must not be done in public and it is not at all amusing; therefore the only thing to do is to hide oneself. Well, so be it."

When he emerged from this "molting time," Vincent's religious fanaticism had disappeared, to be replaced by a burning wrath against the organized Church. "I must tell you that with evangelists it is the same as with artists. There is an old academic school, often detestable, tyrannical, the accumulation of horrors, men who wear a cuirass, a steel armor of prejudices and conventions. . . ." But in rejecting the Church establishment, Vincent only drew closer to the heart of Christianity. "The best way to know God is to love many things. Love a friend, a wife, something—whatever you like—[and] you will be on the way to knowing more about Him; that is what I say to myself. But one must love with a lofty and serious intimate sympathy, with strength, with intelligence. . . ."

It was during his "molting time" in the Borinage that Vincent reached his decision to become an artist. He began by making sketches of the coal-miners and their surroundings, but realized that he was in desperate need of instruction. If he could get an established artist to help him, such a man "would be as one of God's angels to me. I say this in all seriousness and without exaggeration." Accordingly he tried to make contact with someone whose work appealed to him, Jules Breton, a French poet and painter he had met during his days at Goupil's. Breton lived in Courrières, many miles from the Borinage, and Vincent, with only 10 francs in his pocket, had to make the journey on foot. He slept in the open air, "once in an abandoned wagon, which was white with frost the next morning—rather a bad resting place; once in a pile of fagots; and one time that was a little better, in a haystack, where I succeeded in making a rather more comfortable berth—but then a drizzling rain did not exactly further my well-being."

Upon reaching Breton's studio, Vincent was too intimidated by its appearance to knock on the door—the building had what Vincent called "a Methodist regularity." He walked back to the Borinage without seeing Breton, and arrived home, he wrote Theo, "overcome by fatigue, with sore feet, and quite melancholy." But in the depth of his misery he felt his energy revive, "and I said to myself, in spite of everything I shall rise again: I will take up my pencil, which I have forsaken in my great discouragement, and I will go on with my drawing. From that moment everything has seemed transformed for me, and I will go on." Theo, as he always would do, offered to help. Although today there are many altruists-after-the-fact who imagine that they too might have volunteered their aid if they had only been present, the likelihood is that they would have fled at the mere sight of Vincent. He was as poor a risk as ever came straggling down the highroad of art.

The Compassionate Eye

As a young man Vincent van Gogh's strongest compulsion was to love and help mankind. The son of a minister, he chose quite naturally to take up religion. If he had been successful as an evangelist, as he tried to be for several years, he might have drawn and painted as a hobby but he almost surely would not have become an artist. His evangelical mission, however, was a disaster. If anything, he tried too hard. At the age of 25, when he went out to serve the peasants and coal miners of the Borinage, in southern Belgium, his manner was so intense, and his devotion to Christ's teachings so literal, that he antagonized his clerical superiors and probably frightened the people he wanted to help. Although he loved humanity, he could not communicate with individuals and, at 27, he turned to art to communicate for him. It was a logical choice. From childhood, he had made little sketches of ferns, flowers and things around his home. He occasionally illustrated his letters with rough drawings. Furthermore, art was a respected occupation in his family; various uncles—and later his younger brother Theo— were art dealers. But the major reason Van Gogh committed himself to being an artist was that through art he could pour out his feelings. If he could not alleviate the hard life of the poor Dutch peasant, at least he could show his compassion in drawings and paintings. Perhaps this was his way to a communion with God. In any case, it was in this crucible that his art was formed.

Van Gogh's artistic heritage was Dutch. Like the Lowland painters of two centuries earlier, he infused commonplace scenes of Holland with a great sense of their reality— a quality beyond accuracy. This tradition is apparent in the drawing at right—reminiscent of a landscape by Hobbema—in which the figure of a peasant is as securely rooted in the flat countryside as are the tall, bare trees that line his road.

Avenue of Poplars, March 1884

17

"I sometimes think there is nothing so delightful as drawing. This is a fragment . . . of a church bench . . . I saw in a little church in the Geest, where the people from the workhouse go (here they call them very expressively 'orphan men' and 'orphan women')."

"This week I have done a few watercolors out of doors, a little cornfield and a small part of a potato field, and I have also drawn a few landscapes as studies for the surroundings of a few figure drawings I am planning. These are very hasty sketches of those figure drawings. The topmost is the burning of weeds; the other one, the return from the potato field."

18

In his short life Van Gogh wrote nearly a thousand letters, often several a day. Most were written to his brother Theo, possibly the one person in the world who understood him. Only to Theo could Van Gogh describe the impressions and feelings that boiled within him. The letters are extraordinary; literary critics have compared them to the works of the great 19th Century Russian masters of "confessional" writing. But even as he was writing so expressively Van Gogh apparently felt that words were not as vivid as pictures. "Strangely enough," he once wrote Theo, "I sometimes make small sketches almost against my will." Many of these small sketches showed up in his letters. At first they were mostly raw and amateurish, but by 1885, after Van Gogh had been a working artist for five years, they had become powerful miniature art. Excerpts from some of the later illustrated letters to Theo appear here and on the next two pages. The accompanying captions are Van Gogh's.

"The little sketch at the top is what I saw today. . . . In reality, that earth was superb. I don't think my study ripe enough yet, but I was struck by the effect, and as to light and shade, it was indeed as I draw it for you here. The one at the bottom is a tender green little cornfield in the foreground, and withering grasses; behind the cottage, two piles of peat, again a glimpse of heath, and a very light sky."

19

"I am up to my ears in work. Today the almshouse man again posed for a thing that I suddenly felt I had to make before I started anything else. I must tell you that I went to the almshouse again on a visiting day after all. Then I saw the small gardener, and have drawn him from the window. Well, I could not let that go, and I have got as much of it fixed on paper as I can remember."

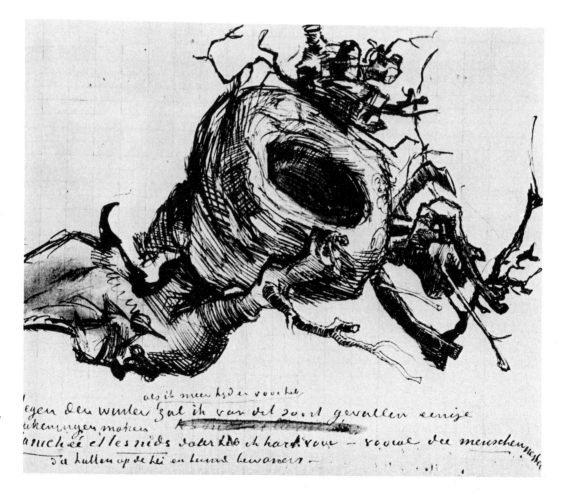

"I think that some people who are good observers of nature might like [my bird's nests] because of the colors of the moss, the dry leaves and the grasses."

"I painted a study . . . on the beach. There are some sea dikes or moles, piers, jetties, and very picturesque ones, too, made of weather-beaten stones and wickerwork. I sat down on one of them and painted the rising tide until it came so near that I had to move my things in a hurry. Between the village and the beach are bushes of a deep bronzed green, tangled by the sea wind. . . . A streetcar is running there now, so it is within easy reach when one has equipment or wet studies to carry home.

"This is a [sketch] of the path to the beach. My thoughts were with you all during the walk."

"If you hear a voice within you saying, 'You are not a painter,' then by all means paint, boy, and that voice will be silenced. . . . One must undertake [work] with confidence, with a certain assurance that one is doing a reasonable thing, like the farmer who drives his plow, or like our friend in the scratch below, who is harrowing, and even drags the harrow himself. If one hasn't a horse, one is one's own horse."

Peasant Woman Tying a Sheaf, summer of 1885

In choosing his early subject matter, Van Gogh scorned the glossy and the showy—the "Cardinal's receptions in Paris," as he put it. In a letter to Theo in April 1885, he wrote, "Painting peasant life is a serious thing and I should reproach myself if I did not try to make pictures which will arouse serious thoughts." The result of that feeling shows in the two figures on these pages. In a drawing of the woman tying a sheaf of straw *(above)*, Van Gogh emphasized the massive hips, the arms as strong as an old tree, the difficult and uncomfortable posture. The woodcutter at right seems as tough and weathered as his crumpled pants. Van Gogh

The Woodcutter, 1885

was intrigued by the clothes of working peasants, for he felt that their faded homespun garments were revealing of their characters; he had no interest in seeing peasants in their "Sunday best." In these drawings he did not even particularize their faces. He wanted to show their human condition, not portray individuals.

Van Gogh was aware of the way these attitudes separated him from his illustrious Dutch predecessors who had also chosen commonplace subjects for their paintings. "The figures in the pictures of the old masters do not *work*," he said. "To draw a peasant's figure in action . . . is the very core of modern art."

After Van Gogh decided on art as his career, he pursued it single-mindedly. Basically self-taught, he did all the necessary exercises to perfect his technique and style. He drew hundreds of detailed studies, like the hands below. He also applied himself to the disciplines of still-life drawing and painting until he could produce stunningly realistic work, like the basket of potatoes at upper right. Van Gogh's control of textures, tones and shapes is so sure that the inert subject somehow seems alive. (Indeed, one art critic wrote that the potatoes "seem to crawl over each other like blind puppies.")

It was after five years of such work that Van Gogh created the masterpiece of his early period, *The Potato Eaters (lower right, and detail on the following pages).* In this painting, all his newly developed technique and experience converged. The people in it are a composite of the many peasants he had seen so compassionately in his years as an evangelist and a beginning artist. But the picture is no generality. In dark, earthen colors he gives witness to the grim life of people to whom dinner consists of stabbing at boiled potatoes in a room as crude as a stable. In details like the gnarled, work-worn hands and coarse features, the tenderness in the eyes of the girl and the glow of orange lamplight, he attests to a harsh but thoroughly human reality. In years to come, Van Gogh's subjects would change—he would seldom again paint such graphic descriptions of the peasant's and the workingman's sorry state. But even in his landscapes, still lifes and portraits he would demonstrate his continuing dedication to a heightened expression of life.

Study of Three Hands, Two Holding a Fork, January-February 1885

Still Life with Potatoes, September 1885

The Potato Eaters, April-May 1885

II

A Mission
in Art

Van Gogh painted this view of
Paris from a window of the
apartment he shared with Theo in
the Montmartre section of the city.
His use of short brush strokes
shows the influence of Seurat's
Pointillism, which he had studied
during the year. The red shutters,
blue rooftops, pale yellow buildings
and gray-green sky hues mark a
permanent departure from his dark
Dutch palette—and foretell the
brilliant colors of his future work.

*View across Paris, from Vincent's
Room,* Paris, 1887

Having decided at long last—at 27—that his mission in life was to become an artist, Van Gogh established his first "studio" in the cottage
of a Borinage coal miner. He paid the rent with small sums sent by his father and commenced his education in a "rage of work." From Paris,
Theo forwarded sheaves of prints for him to study and copy, and from
The Hague the manager of Goupil's branch office sent textbooks on anat-
omy and perspective. But Vincent soon found his quarters so dim and
cramped—his "studio" was actually a bedroom that he shared with the
miner's children—that he was often obliged to work outdoors. With
the onset of autumn it became apparent that he would have to find
other lodgings. Theo suggested that Vincent join him in Paris, but Vincent seems to have been reluctant to venture into what was then the center of the art world. Instead, in the fall of 1880, he went to Brussels
and moved into the cheapest hotel he could find.

"My chief food," he wrote Theo, "is dry bread and some potatoes or
chestnuts which people sell here on the street corners." The reference
to his diet may have merely been intended to assure Theo that he was
not living in luxury, but it is worth note. During most of his adult life
Vincent was severely undernourished. Even when he had money for
food, he preferred to spend it on models and art supplies. He once remarked that he had "lived mainly for four days on 23 cups of coffee,"
and inevitably, despite his powerful constitution, his health broke down.
He may have suffered from one of the vitamin-deficiency diseases—perhaps a mild form of pellagra—for in his early thirties his teeth began to
break off and he was obliged to wear a false set.

Vincent remained in Brussels during the winter of 1880-1881, la-
boriously struggling with his draftsmanship and reporting his progress
to Theo. At the time Theo, a rising young businessman, was involved
in the reorganization of Goupil's Paris gallery and failed to answer Vincent's letters by return post. Vincent after several months became angry
and spiteful. "I must say," he wrote, "it seems rather strange and un-
accountable that you have not written me since the one letter I received
on my arrival here. . . . In thinking of you, I unconsciously ask my-

self, Why doesn't he write? If he is afraid of compromising himself in the eyes of Messrs. Goupil & Cie. by keeping in touch with me—is his position with those gentlemen so shaky and unstable that he is obliged to be so careful? Or is it that he is afraid that I will ask him for money? But if this was the reason for your silence, you might at least have waited until I tried to squeeze something out of you, as the saying goes."

Theo did not reply in kind, and within a month the truth emerged. The money ostensibly coming from home was actually being supplied by Theo. "I hear from Father," wrote Vincent, "that without my knowing it you have been sending me money for a long time. . . . Accept my heartfelt thanks, I firmly believe you will not regret it." Vincent's gratitude and his agonized sense of dependence on his brother were later a constant theme in his letters. Occasionally the dependence galled him, and he lashed out bitterly at the mild, hard-working Theo. But in time he reached the view that his brother should receive partial credit for his paintings, as though he had shared in their creation. And when Vincent committed suicide, one of the precipitating factors seems to have been his feeling that he had somehow failed Theo, and could no longer accept his support.

In Brussels, through an introduction supplied by Theo, Vincent made the acquaintance of a wealthy young painter named Anton van Rappard, an amiable but insignificant artist. Van Rappard was at first startled by Vincent, who was inclined to stop and stare at peasants laboring in the fields, and to shout, "How shall I ever manage to paint what I love so much?" But Van Rappard soon realized that he was dealing with an extraordinary man and offered such help as he could—although his teaching was limited largely to fundamentals. Vincent, in fact, was essentially self-taught. Even though he occasionally sought help from other artists and at times even attended formal art classes, he could never abide for long the discipline of established authority. This is not to imply that he was a "primitive." On the contrary, the distortions in perspective and the exuberance of color in his mature paintings are not in the least inadvertent; they are the exquisitely calculated departures from long-accepted ideas of a man solidly grounded in his craft.

Despite Theo's help, Vincent's living expenses in Brussels soon proved to be too great. To save money he decided to spend the summer in his parents' house at Etten, but he was uncertain of his reception. "I am willing to give in about dress or anything else to suit them," he wrote Theo. Even so, he expected to be misjudged: "I blame no one for it, because relatively few people know why an artist acts as he does. But in general, he who searches all kinds of places to find picturesque spots or figures—holes and corners that another passes by—is accused of many bad intentions and villainies that have never entered his head. A peasant who sees me draw an old tree trunk, and sees me sitting there for an hour, thinks I have gone mad and . . . laughs at me." Nevertheless in April 1881, a few weeks after his 28th birthday, he went to Etten with modest hopes.

At first all went well, and Vincent hurled himself into his work with the ferocious energy that marked his entire career. "I have drawn five times over a man with a spade . . . in different positions, a sower twice, a girl with a broom twice. Then a woman in a white cap, peeling potatoes; a shepherd leaning on his staff. . . . I now no longer stand helpless before nature, as I used to do." Nevertheless, his progress was slow. Among the drawings from this period one of the most memorable is that of *The Sower*—memorable not for its skill, but for its air of imminent explosion. The wooden-shoed peasant, his head too large, his arms too short, and on his face a look of angry desperation, seems about to scatter his apronful of seed in a motion of spastic convulsion.

The theme of *The Sower* doubtless came to Vincent from one of his major artistic idols, Jean-François Millet. But unlike the French painter, who ennobled and sentimentalized peasant labor, Vincent was already groping toward an expression of kinship, anger and ruthless reality that Millet never attained. In the hope that *The Sower* and other pictures like it might be salable, Vincent around this time indulged in one of his few small vanities—he signed some of his drawings "Atelier Vincent." But he soon enough found out that there was no market for pictures of peasants that were not, as he put it, "perfumed."

Vincent had been home for only a few months when there occurred the second of his catastrophic affairs with women. In his letters he referred to her only as Kee. Her full name was Kee Vos and she was his first cousin, the daughter of an Amsterdam preacher named Jan Stricker. Recently widowed, accompanied by her four-year-old son, she had come to spend a vacation in the Van Gogh parsonage to recover her morale. Vincent soon fell deeply in love with her. He courted her obliquely by befriending her little boy, and Kee came to regard him as a gentle, eccentric relative. When he suddenly announced his passion for her, she was dumfounded. No doubt in the belief that it was the most charitable reply she could give him, she told him that she never intended to marry again. But Vincent could not accept this, and pressed his case with such frightening intensity that Kee in a panic cried out, "No, never, never!"

Van Gogh's second disastrous affair of the heart was with Kee Vos, a widow he met in Etten in 1881. Kee had so loved her husband that she was overcome with grief when he died. Vincent's efforts to amuse her young son while she was mourning touched her, but she was quite unprepared for his ardent advances. "He was so kind to my little boy," Kee Vos said. "He fancied that he loved me." When Vincent blurted out his feelings to the widow, Kee fled home to her parents.

Vincent refused to believe that the "No, never, never!" was final. His letters to Theo were filled with anatomizations of love. He would, he wrote, clasp Kee to his breast as though she were a block of ice, and melt her, "for love is something so positive, so strong, so real that it is as impossible for one who loves to take back that feeling as it is to take his own life." Kee, for her part, fled to Amsterdam and, when he wrote her, refused to open any of his letters. Vincent then turned his frustration against his parents. "As you know," he wrote Theo, "Father and Mother on one side and I on the other do not agree about what must be done or not done in regard to a certain 'no, never, never.' Well, after hearing the rather strong expressions 'indelicate' and 'untimely' for some time (just imagine that you were in love and they called your love indelicate, would you not have proudly resented it and said, Stop!), I emphatically requested that these expressions not be used any more. . . . Now they say I am 'breaking family ties.'"

Theo tried to discourage Vincent, without success. Bursting with love, Vincent solicited the help of his covey of aunts and uncles, but succeeded only in alarming them. At length Theo sent him the money for a ticket to Amsterdam and Vincent journeyed there to confront the frightened young widow. Her parents do not seem to have been equipped to cope with the visitation, and Kee was even less so. Hearing or glimpsing Vincent as he appeared at the front door, she dashed out the back one. What followed is not wholly clear: Vincent's existing letters on the subject do not tell the whole story. Apparently he insisted on seeing Kee, and when he was told that this was impossible, thrust his hand into the flame of a lamp, demanding to speak to her for only so long as he could endure the pain. Horrified, the Strickers blew out the lamp, and Vincent may have fainted—at all events, he later told Theo, "everything became a blank." When he came to, Kee's parents, in a gesture that rings so true to life that most fiction writers would reject it, took Vincent in charge. With every reason to fear and dislike him, they insisted on finding him good lodgings. "And, dear me, those two old people went with me through the cold, foggy, muddy streets and they did indeed show me a very good, cheap inn."

Kee's rejection of him only increased Vincent's desire for human warmth and companionship. "I . . . felt chilled through and through, to the depths of my soul," he wrote Theo. "And I did not want to be stunned by that feeling." Instead of returning directly to Etten, he detoured briefly to The Hague and found himself a prostitute. He admitted that it was illogical, in view of his vehement insistence upon having Kee and no other, but "Who is the master, the logic or I?" In any case, he said, he could not do otherwise. "I need a woman, I cannot, I will not live without love. I am a man and a man with passions. I must go to a woman, otherwise I shall freeze or turn to stone." When he got back to Etten he remained for only a short time. The misunderstandings and quarrels with his father became more frequent. Soon he resolved to break off relations and move to The Hague, where he might study with Anton Mauve, a prominent Dutch painter of the day who had married one of Vincent's cousins. With Mauve to guide him he could learn more about art than he ever could in a country parsonage. His departure was bitter—he chose Christmas Day to denounce the organized Church to his father, saying "straight out that I considered the whole system abominable."

Theo was shocked. He thought Vincent's decision to settle in The Hague sensible enough, but could not approve the manner of his going. He wrote Vincent a blistering letter: "That you could not bear it there any longer is possible, and that you differ in opinion with people who have lived all their lives in the country and have not come in contact with modern life is not unnatural; but, confound it, what made you so childish and impudent as to embitter and spoil Father's and Mother's life in that way?" Vincent replied in a long, defensive essay in which he admitted that his "diplomacy" had been swept away in the heat of the moment. As to a reconciliation with his father, he merely sent the old man a New Year's greeting in which he said that he hoped they would have no more trouble in the next 12 months.

At first Mauve was sympathetic to Vincent. He gave him some paints and brushes, helped him to set up a studio, introduced him into an artists' association where he could draw from models, and was generous with technical advice. But Mauve, although he was a skilled and sensitive painter whose work was distinguished for its delicate color, could not long abide so unorthodox a pupil as Vincent. When he criticized Vincent's drawings and advised him to practice by sketching from plaster casts, Vincent responded by smashing the casts in a coalbox and proclaiming that it was life he wanted to draw, not cold plaster. To Mauve such behavior was unacceptable; he told Vincent he would be too busy to see him for two months.

Vincent's experience with other would-be benefactors was similar. One of his art-dealing uncles, Cornelius van Gogh, visited him and bought a few of his drawings for the equivalent of one dollar apiece. He promised to buy more if Vincent would only concentrate on salable subjects—pretty views of tourist attractions, for instance. The manager of the local branch of Goupil's came to him with much the same offer. Vincent tried, but the work did not interest him in the least and he was very soon attacking these men as unfeeling creatures with no conception of true art. He was right, but his inflexible principles brought him only posthumous benefits and paid no rent and purchased no bread or coffee in this world. Vincent has been called a modern saint, and the idea may not be too far off the mark—bearing in mind that saints are frequently unbending, infuriating men who invite their own martyrdom.

Van Gogh's view of his profession, which he formulated in The Hague, was in fact a saintly one. "I want you to understand clearly my conception of art," he wrote Theo. "What I want and aim at is confoundedly difficult, and yet I do not think I aim too high. I want to do drawings which *touch* some people. . . . In either figure or landscape I should wish to express, not sentimental melancholy, but serious sorrow. . . . I want to progress so far that people will say of my work, he feels deeply, he feels tenderly—notwithstanding my so-called roughness, perhaps even because of it. . . . What am I in most people's eyes? A nonentity, or an eccentric and disagreeable man—somebody who has no position in society and never will have, in short, the lowest of the low. Very well . . . then I should want my work to show what is in the heart of such an eccentric, of such a nobody. This is my ambition, which is, in spite of everything, founded less on anger than on love."

If Mauve and Uncle Cornelius and the branch manager of Goupil's had seen this side of Vincent they might have understood it. Unfortunately they saw something else. Soon after his arrival in The Hague, Vincent had resumed his contact with the prostitute he had sought out when Kee had rejected him. Her name was Christien—nicknamed Sien—and by all accounts she would have struck fear into the heart of a drunken stevedore. She was 30, and had been in her profession for about 15 years. Smallpox had pitted her face; she was addicted to alcohol, smoked cigars, spoke in coarse, raucous accents and had a scheming procuress for a mother. She had already borne one illegitimate child, was pregnant with another, and appears to have had gonorrhea into the bargain.

After Kee Vos rejected him, Van Gogh found solace with a streetwalker called Sien. In the spring of 1883 he made this charcoal drawing of his mistress and her 11-year-old daughter. Van Gogh rhapsodized Sien to his brother, even when both were hospitalized, she pregnant, he with gonorrhea. And the preachments of his father ("Bad connections often arise from a feeling of loneliness") only goaded Vincent to flaunt his contempt for people "who attach importance to refinement and outward form." But after a year and a half, Van Gogh and Sien parted: he went to paint in the countryside; she returned to a brothel.

Vincent made several studies of her—the most arresting is a lithograph with the title *Sorrow* written boldly on the page.

Although he informed Theo that he had found some inexpensive models—the prostitute, her mother and her daughter, aged about 11—Vincent did not at first reveal the nature of his relationship with them. This lack of candor, exceedingly rare in his letters, may have arisen from Vincent's anxiety not to lose his only life line—the 100 francs (about $20) a month that Theo sent him from Paris. If so, Vincent underestimated Theo. At length, however, it became necessary to bring the affair to light. Mauve, Uncle Cornelius and others knew about it, and were accusing Vincent of "betraying" his family and his social class: "You have a vicious character," said Mauve.

Aware that word would soon reach Theo, Vincent seized the initiative. "Which is more delicate, refined, manly," he wrote his brother, "to desert a woman or to stand by a forsaken woman? Last winter I met a pregnant woman, deserted by the man whose child she carried. A pregnant woman who had to walk the streets in winter, had to earn her bread, you understand how. . . . I could not pay her the full wages of a model, but that did not prevent my paying her rent, and thank God, so far I have been able to protect her and her child from hunger and cold by sharing my own bread with her. . . . It seems to me that every man worth a straw would have done the same in such a case. . . . The woman is now attached to me like a tame dove. For my part, I can only marry once, and how can I do better than marry her? It is the only way to help her; otherwise misery would force her back into her old ways, which end in a precipice."

Theo argued strongly against the marriage, but Vincent insisted on it and planned to wed Sien as soon as her baby was born. However, several weeks before the child arrived, Vincent himself entered the hospital to be treated for gonorrhea. It was months before he was wholly well again, and although in time he did install Sien and her child—a boy—in a sparsely furnished apartment, and wrote rapturously to Theo of his "house" and his "family," he never took the final step of marrying her. Perhaps Theo's arguments had begun to take effect; perhaps Vincent himself had begun to see the difficulties of marriage with a woman whose conversation did not extend much beyond oaths. In any case, although he continued to live with Sien for many months, her name appeared in his letters less and less frequently.

Meanwhile he continued to make progress with his art. In a letter to Theo he described an ingenious device he was using to help him master perspective—a frame with four threads stretched across it, one horizontal, one vertical and two diagonal. (The idea was not new—Albrecht Dürer had used a similar frame in the 16th Century.) Placing the frame before his subject and sighting through the threads made it easier for Vincent to render spatial effects—lines of perspective and foreshortening—more convincingly. "The lines of roofs and gutters now come shooting forth powerfully," he wrote, "like arrows from a bow." He was also beginning to pay serious heed to experiments in oil, and he spoke of these more eloquently than artists ordinarily do.

"In the woods, yesterday toward evening," he wrote Theo, "I was busy painting a rather sloping ground covered with dry, moldered beech leaves. This ground was light and dark reddish-brown, made more so by the shadows of trees casting more or less dark streaks over it, sometimes half blotted out. The problem was—and I found it very difficult—to get the depth of color, the enormous force and solidity of that ground —and while painting it I perceived for the very first time how much light there still was in that dusk. . . . Behind those saplings, behind that brownish-red soil, is a sky very delicate, bluish-gray, warm, hardly blue, all aglow. . . . A few figures of wood gatherers are wandering around like dark masses of mysterious shadows. The white cap of a woman bending to reach a dry branch stands out suddenly. . . . A skirt catches the light. . . . A white bonnet, a cap, a shoulder, the bust of a woman molds itself against the sky. Those figures are large and full of poetry. . . .

"While painting it I said to myself, I must not go away before there is something of an autumn evening in it, something mysterious, something serious. But as this effect does not last, I had to paint quickly. The figures were put in at once with a few strong strokes of a firm brush. It struck me how sturdily those little [sapling] stems were rooted in the ground. I began painting them with a brush, but because the surface was already so heavily covered, a brush stroke was lost in it— then I squeezed the roots and trunks in from the tube, and modeled it a little with the brush. Yes—now they stand there rising from the ground, strongly rooted in it. . . . In a certain way I am glad that I have not *learned* painting, because then I might have *learned* to pass by such effects as this."

It was Vincent's instinct, in his haste to get great quantities of paint onto the canvas, to squeeze colors directly from the tube. In his later work his impasto is often so thick that the paintings, in profile, seem

In a letter to his brother, Van Gogh described his design for a wooden "perspective frame," rigged with four taut strings, which he used as an aid to composition *(below, left)*. "In the meadows one can look through it like a window. Long and continuous practice with it enables one to draw quick as lightning." In another letter, he drew a diagram of the way he arranged his pigments on the palette *(below, right)*. "You will understand that I limited myself to the simple colors," he wrote, "ocher (red-yellow-brown), cobalt and Prussian blue, Naples yellow, sienna, black and white. . . . I refrained from choosing 'nice' colors. . . . I believe this is a practical palette with healthy colors."

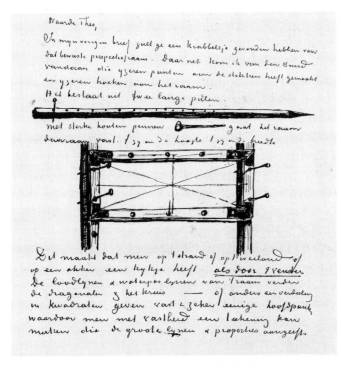

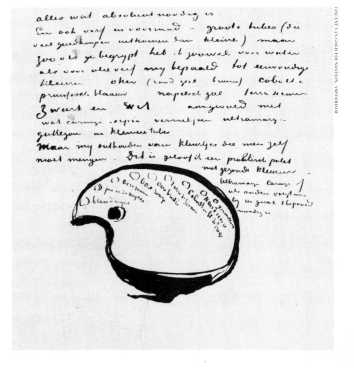

Van Gogh drew this view of his family's home in Nuenen after he returned to live with his parents in 1883. The laundry room he was using as a studio is at the right. His parents had put a stove in it and had covered the stone floor with planks to protect him from the winter damp. They even talked of cutting a large window in one wall to make the room lighter and airier. But Vincent did not want this done and it was not long before he found a studio of his own elsewhere in Nuenen.

like topographical studies, the ridges of pigment rising almost half an inch above the surface. And in his last years, when he produced canvases in prodigious numbers and they were stacked together for storage, these little mountaintops of paint were sometimes accidentally flattened where parts of one painting had pressed down on the face of the one below.

Although Vincent's description of the evening scene shows his effort to cope with color—the dusk, the brownish-red earth, bluish-gray sky— the fact is that his early color harmonies were all subdued, in the manner of the standard dark Dutch palette of his time. There was nothing in Holland to compare with the brilliant colorism of the French Impressionists. Vincent, thinking himself daring, spoke of being unafraid "of a bright green or a soft blue," but then denied this boldness by remarking that "there is scarcely any color that is not gray: red-gray, yellow-gray, green-gray, blue-gray. This is the substance of the whole color scheme." In a short time he would think otherwise.

Despite the strides he made in his work, Vincent remained trapped in his relationship with Sien. He would not abandon her—she and her children were indeed his family, and beyond that were the symbols of poor, helpless humanity on whom he could not turn his back. But if saints have their difficult side, so do the poor. Sien wanted more than Vincent could provide. Although Theo had increased his monthly stipend to 150 francs, and had begun to send it in installments at 10-day intervals in the hope that Vincent might manage it better, it was not enough. Sien's mother began to pressure her to leave Vincent and get a good steady job—in a bordello. There was a brief tug-of-war between Sien's mother and Vincent; he lost. Nevertheless, he continued to defend Sien. "How can she be good when she has never known good?" he asked. He blamed himself for failing to uplift her—he had somehow been inadequate.

In the upshot he decided to leave The Hague and go to Drenthe, a province in the peat-bog region of northern Holland where he felt he might

"This garden sets me dreaming," Vincent wrote from the Nuenen parsonage in March 1884, and his feeling for the family home shows in this drawing of the grounds. In the background stands Nuenen's old tower, a landmark in the little village. Vincent spent most of his days making such sketches of his surroundings and the village folk. He dined with his family, but during meals he would often crouch in a corner with his plate balanced on his knees, staring silently at a drawing he had propped on a chair.

deepen his art by drawing closer to the peasants and the earth. Before his departure he gave Sien the only gift he could—a piece of painter's canvas from which to make clothing for her children. He also wrote to Theo, in a matter-of-fact manner, that he had estimated his own chances of survival and thought that he might still count on a little while. As to years, he estimated the number "between six and ten," and he was accurate. He had seven. "I do *not* intend to spare myself, nor to avoid emotions or difficulties—I don't care much whether I live a longer or shorter time. . . . The world concerns me only insofar as I feel a certain indebtedness and duty toward it because I have walked this earth for thirty years, and, out of gratitude, want to leave some souvenir in the shape of drawings or pictures—not made to please a certain taste in art, but to express a sincere human feeling."

His sojourn in Drenthe was brief—only two months—and not notably productive. He was tortured by guilt for having "abandoned" Sien, he lacked painting materials, and he found the peasants unwilling to pose for him. Late in 1883 he decided to make one more attempt to live with his parents. His father at the time was serving in Nuenen, and despite all past quarrels, was more than willing to take him in—he spent his limited funds to make a small studio for Vincent in an unused laundry room. The quarrels of course resumed, but a kind of armed truce was established, and Vincent worked furiously on landscapes, still lifes and pictures of the Nuenen peasants—particularly of the local weavers in their cottages, who seemed to him not to be in control of their heavy looms, but victims caught in spiderwebs or in bizarre, Inquisitional devices of torture. His colors were still dark—he compared them to "soft [green] soap and the brass color of a worn-out 10-centime piece."

In March 1885, in a letter to Theo, Pastor van Gogh spoke of another of his failed attempts to establish communication with Vincent, and added philosophically, "May he meet with success in something, no matter what." Two days later, returning from a long walk, the pastor collapsed at his front door and died. He was 63. Vincent, who could not pretend what he did not feel, referred to his father's death in the briefest of terms, and went on to tell Theo of his plans to start a composition of "those peasants around a dish of potatoes in the evening." "Those peasants" was a subject that stirred Vincent deeply; a worn-out, conservative preacher, fallen dead on his doorstep, represented only the pathetic, not the tragic—what Vincent had earlier called "sentimental melancholy" as opposed to "serious sorrow."

The Potato Eaters (pages 25-27) is ordinarily called Van Gogh's first "masterpiece"—whatever that threadbare word may now mean. It is the statement and the indictment toward which he had been tending all his life, and his own comments best describe his intent: "I have tried to emphasize that these people, eating their potatoes in the lamplight, have dug the earth with those very hands they put in the dish, and so it speaks of *manual labor*, and how they have honestly earned their food.

"I have wanted to give the impression of a way of life quite different from that of us civilized people. Therefore I am not at all anxious for everyone to like it or admire it at once. . . . I personally am convinced I get better results by painting them in their roughness than by giving them a conventional charm.

"I think a peasant girl is more beautiful than a lady, in her dusty, patched blue skirt and bodice. . . . If a peasant picture smells of bacon, smoke, potato steam—all right, that's not unhealthy; if a stable smells of dung—all right, that belongs to a stable; if the field has an odor of ripe corn or potatoes or of guano or manure—that's healthy."

There are no references to religion in Vincent's remarks about *The Potato Eaters*, yet it is a religious painting of the most powerful sort. It is at once a vision of a sacrament—the communion of those who toil—and an accusation; it is intended to arouse guilt and wrath among "us civilized people" who tolerate, or profit from, human degradation. Although he never put his political views into a formal statement, Vincent was a man of the left, deeply moved by the novels of Émile Zola and Victor

In the first seven months of 1884, Van Gogh did 10 paintings and 17 drawings and watercolors of weavers—men who to him seemed literally enmeshed in their looms as they worked inside their gloomy cottages. "If you put my study next to the drawing of a loom by a man who specializes in draftsmanship," Van Gogh wrote, "my work would show that the oak of the loom had become dingy and aged-looking from sweaty hands. . . . Compare it with a real loom and mine will creak more! The miners and the weavers still constitute a race apart from other laborers and artisans, and I feel a great sympathy for them. With his dreamy air . . . almost a sleepwalker—that is the weaver."

Hugo and by his own observations in the slums, the coal mines and peasant hovels. One of his lifelong dreams was to establish a commune of artists where painters could share their lives and their fortunes—a commune having more to do with early Christianity than with Marxist theory. He also proposed a plan for bringing fine works of art into the homes of the poor, through lithographs, at no more than a few cents a print—and he saw this not as a commercial enterprise, but as a duty. Art for him had primarily a social function, although to be sure it was also the only language in which he could plead for the love that was otherwise denied him.

Eight months after his father's death Vincent left Holland, never to return. He went first to Antwerp, where he again enrolled in formal art classes. His fellow pupils remembered him as a country clod who dressed in rough peasant clothes and used a board from a packing crate for a palette. When his instructors asked him his name, he replied simply "Well, I am Vincent, a Dutchman." He derived very little from his classes beyond the reinforcement of his conviction that academies are an abomination. The principal benefit of his three-month sojourn in Antwerp was an increased exposure to color, or, more accurately, increased thought about it.

Van Gogh, who was soon to be the most intense colorist of his time, was by no means oblivious to the possibilities of color during his Dutch period. He was familiar with the color theories of the great French painter Delacroix and seems even by this period to have begun to develop the almost mystical ideas about color that are reflected in his late art. He sensed that color has meaning that transcends mere visual impressions. Yellow, red, blue—indeed any color—can connote something that lies beyond the reach of rationality. Precisely what the connotation may be is a complex matter that scientists and cultural historians have not yet penetrated, but it is a commonplace that colors and emotions are interrelated; without thinking of it, one speaks of a red rage, a blue mood, or being green with envy. Vincent himself, before he left Holland, went so far as to relate colors and music—and even took a few piano lessons. "Prussian blue!" or "Chrome yellow!" he would cry as he struck a chord, no doubt alarming the piano teacher, although he was merely experimenting with a phenomenon that artists and musicians have always known about.

In Antwerp Vincent studied the bright colors of Rubens in the museums and in the city's churches, and was impressed. His own paintings began to take on lighter tones, and he added scarlet, cadmium yellow and emerald green to his palette. After a few months he seems to have sensed that his art was about to undergo a great change, and that he was at last ready to go to Paris. He suggested the idea to Theo, who was apprehensive and tried to discourage him. It was no use. One day in February 1886 Theo was handed a note scrawled in black chalk; Vincent was waiting for him in the magnificent Salon Carré of the Louvre, where the wonders of the world—Leonardos, Rembrandts and all that is best in the realm of painting—confronted one another. Would Theo please meet him there?

The Impact of Paris

When Van Gogh arrived in Paris, on a brisk February morning in 1886, he was eager to learn and ready to be stimulated by new experiences. Paris in that year was the place to be. The city bubbled with innovations in science, literature, music and, most excitingly perhaps, in art. For the first time, Van Gogh was exposed to the world of Manet, Degas, Cézanne, the Impressionists, the Pointillists, the Symbolists, Japanese art—and everything else of interest around town that his brother Theo and the young art leaders could show him. Still shy and reclusive, Vincent nevertheless became friendly with Pissarro, Toulouse-Lautrec, Signac, Gauguin and other avant-garde painters, examining their work and their ideas intently. At his easel, he filtered all his sensations through his vibrant brush. In two years he went through a complete metamorphosis as a painter. He had described himself as a "shaggy dog" when he was in Holland doing the somber *Potato Eaters;* in Paris he turned into what one critic has called a "singing bird." Brightness and lightness flooded his work. He painted serene café interiors and breeze-swept landscapes. The dark figures of laborers at work were replaced by vivid close-ups of friends *(right)* and of himself at rest. The gaiety and stimulation of Paris' art world did not alter Van Gogh's basic personality; he had arrived from Holland with eccentric and disturbing character traits, and he kept them all through his life. But Paris liberated his massive creative power.

In Vincent's portrait, the art supply dealer Père Tanguy, painted in deep blues and browns, sits against a bold background composed mostly of Van Gogh's copies of Japanese works. Van Gogh's affectionate portrayal also includes a touch of whimsy. Although the kind Tanguy was a champion of unrecognized artists, apparently his wife did not appreciate the fact that most of them owed him money. The erupting volcano in the painting directly above his head is said to be Van Gogh's comment on Tanguy's married life.

Père Tanguy, 1887

Coming from Holland, where painters still confined themselves more or less to traditional techniques, Van Gogh in Paris suddenly found himself looking at pictures like these. New painting styles that he had known only through Theo's descriptions now became excitingly real. He probably became quite familiar with most of the paintings shown here. Theo, a forward-looking art dealer, had already begun collecting "modern" works. At one time he owned many of the pictures in this group—those by Manet, Seurat, Gauguin, Toulouse-Lautrec and Émile Bernard—and Vincent lived surrounded by them when he shared Theo's apartment. Also close at hand were the galleries where the Impressionists held their exhibitions; equally accessible was Père Tanguy's shop, where many pictures, including the Cézanne shown here, were for sale. As he became a member of the group of progressive young artists, Vincent not only observed many of them at work in their studios but sometimes joined them in painting expeditions out of doors.

Édouard Manet: *Portrait*, c. 1880

Paul Cézanne: *Mill on the Couleure near Pontoise*, c. 1881

Edgar Degas: *After the Bath*, c. 1885

Georges Seurat: *A Café-Concert*, 1887

Claude Monet: *A Field of Poppies*, 1873

Camille Pissarro: *Landscape at the Chaponval*, 1880

Paul Signac: *The Dining Room (Breakfast)*, 1886-1887

Pierre-Auguste Renoir: *The Bathers*, 1884-1887

Paul Gauguin: *At the Pond*, date unknown

Henri de Toulouse-Lautrec: *Woman at a Table*, 1889

Émile Bernard: *Portrait of the Artist's Grandmother*, 1887

A Woman in the Café Le Tambourin, 1887

44

Van Gogh absorbed many of the new techniques to which he was exposed in Paris by deliberately imitating them in his own work. Below is one of his exercises in Pointillism: for the café interior he painted the walls and, to a lesser extent, the floor in distinct dots of pure color. In his copy of a Japanese wood-block print *(left)*, he practiced painting with solid areas of color, hard outlines and flattened perspective. At the far left is his version of one of the traditional Impressionist subjects, a woman alone in a café. His model may have been La Segatori, the Italian who owned the café Le Tambourin; his borrowed technique is revealed in the short, slashing brush strokes of pure color that make the table, the chairs and the model's hat especially vivid. It was to decorate this café that Van Gogh painted some of his Japanese pictures, and it was here that he exhibited a collection of Japanese prints.

Japonaiserie: Trees in Bloom, 1887

Interior of a Restaurant, 1887

Wheat Field with a Lark, June-July 1887

In Paris, Van Gogh freed his palette of the dark, earth tones he had used in most of his early work in Holland, refined his technique of modeling forms in light and shadow, and painted portraits, flower studies and landscapes instead of depressed peasants. These were revolutionary changes for him and he worked vigorously to master them: some 200 paintings flowed from his brush inside two years, about 50 of flowers, some 35 still lifes and half a hundred landscapes. As he progressed in these new methods, some of the earthy reality of his Dutch peasant paintings began to reassert itself. The two landscapes shown here demonstrate his absorption in Impressionism but they also carry overtones of that earlier work. The painting above, for example, owes its colors to Impressionism. It is an Impressionist device to let the brush stroke itself play a part in the object the stroke represents, as Van Gogh does with the shafts of wheat and the red flecks of the flowers. But by placing the main elements of the picture—grass, wheat and sky —in strong horizontal bands, he seems to plant the delicate scene as solidly in the earth as the thick Dutch trees he painted previously. And in the picture at the right, the figure with the spade echoes the Dutch peasants of his earlier work, just as the subject—a windmill he found in the Montmartre section of Paris— is a reminder of the windmills of his native land.

46

Windmill on Montmartre, 1887

III

Pilgrimage to Paris

Although Vincent was 32 when he came to Paris in 1886, and Theo only 28, the roles of the two brothers had long since been reversed. Theo was the senior in all but years. In appearance he much resembled Vincent, but in manner he was quite the opposite: a gentle and self-effacing man who moved softly in the world of Parisian art. Even those with good cause to remember him failed to develop a sharp impression. Paul Gauguin, for whom Theo did substantial favors, never bothered to master the spelling of his name, writing of him as "van Gog." The French poet Gustave Kahn saw him as "pale, blond and so melancholy that he seemed to hold canvases the way beggars hold their wooden bowls. His profound conviction of the value of the new art was stated without vigor, and thus without great success. He did not have a barker's gift. But this salesman was an excellent critic and engaged in discussions with painters and writers as the discriminating art lover he was." Neither Kahn nor Gauguin made note of Theo's unspectacular courage.

In his 13 years with Goupil & Cie. Theo had risen to the managership of one of the two galleries the firm maintained in Paris. It was the smaller gallery, but Theo was authorized to buy and sell paintings at his discretion. For sound business reasons the pictures he put on prominent display were recognized masters, such as Corot. But upstairs and in his storage racks he kept a large number of paintings by less well-known artists whose work he admired. When he collapsed with a nervous breakdown after Vincent's suicide and his conservative employers had to replace him, they were outraged to discover the extent of his extraordinary purchases. "Theo van Gogh," one of them told Theo's successor, "has accumulated the most appalling stuff by modern painters. . . . Just do the best you can with them and don't bother us, or we'll be obliged to close the place down." The successor's inventory disclosed what would today be regarded as a priceless art collection—works by Gauguin, Degas, Pissarro, Daumier, Redon and Toulouse-Lautrec. At various times Theo also bought canvases from Monet, Renoir and Sisley, painters who have since been installed in the pantheon of

Van Gogh, sitting at a café table, was portrayed in pastel by Henri de Toulouse-Lautrec the year after he met the Dutchman in Paris. Although the younger Lautrec was already an accomplished artist on his own, he seems to have been influenced by Van Gogh's power and intensity, the effect of which can be seen here in the bold colors and closely knit, hatched strokes.

Henri de Toulouse-Lautrec:
Portrait of Vincent van Gogh,
Paris, 1887

modern art. Few dealers in history have had a more discerning eye.

Theo did not relish the prospect of sharing his small apartment with Vincent, who could create squalor with a wave of the hand. But he made room for his brother, and undertook first of all to repair Vincent's health. Although he had not yet begun to drink heavily, years of self-neglect had brought Vincent to the brink of physical and nervous collapse. Theo paid for the services of a doctor and a dentist, and did his best to point out the advantages of food. As soon as he was able, he rented a larger apartment on the Rue Lepic in Montmartre, with an extra room that could serve Vincent as a studio. Thereafter he wrote optimistically to their mother in Holland: "We are getting along well in the new flat; you would not recognize Vincent, he has changed so much, and other people find it even more striking than I do. . . . The doctor says that he is now hale and hearty again. He is making tremendous progress in his work and is beginning to succeed. He is also far more cheerful than before, and is very well liked. For example, he has some friends who each week send him a nice consignment of flowers for him to paint. He paints mainly flowers, above all in order to freshen up his colors for future paintings. If we can keep it up, then I think he has the worst behind him; and he is going to come out on top."

Although Vincent's temperament prevented him from being "well liked" for very long—he had a calamitous habit of shouting out his opinion—it is true that in Paris, for the first and only time in his life, he did associate with a number of other artists on a friendly basis. Many of them he met in art class where, surprisingly, he enrolled almost immediately after his arrival. His teacher was Fernand Cormon, an academic painter of minor talent who had built a reputation on large pictures of prehistoric lake dwellers and cavemen. Thin as a sparrow, with a sparrow's face, Cormon was held in awe by his pupils, perhaps not so much for his paintings as for the fact that he kept three mistresses at one time.

At Cormon's, Vincent worked hard to perfect his technical skill. Although he had previously expressed his contempt for making studies from plaster casts, he now proceeded to do precisely that, drawing, redrawing and erasing with such zeal that he rubbed holes in the paper. He was considerably older than the other pupils and his perception was unlike theirs—in his new-found fascination with color he saw an ordinary nude against a dull background as golden-yellow against bright blue. No one was inclined to ridicule him, however, possibly because of his touching earnestness but more likely because he seemed frightening. Archibald Hartrick, a British painter who knew him at the time, recalled that "he had an extraordinary way of pouring out sentences, if he got started, in Dutch, English and French, then glancing back at you over his shoulder, and hissing through his teeth." (Hartrick made a sketch of Vincent in this attitude.)

Like many of Vincent's enthusiasms, his desire to study with Cormon quickly burned out. He entered the class announcing that he intended to stay for three years but left after a few weeks. The chief benefit of his sessions there seems to have been his introduction to a num-

Theo van Gogh, four years Vincent's junior, looked more the artist than his brother. "He was more delicately built," Theo's wife recalled, "and his features were more refined, but he had the same reddish fair complexion and the same light blue eyes which sometimes darkened to a greenish blue." In a letter to Theo, Vincent once asserted that "certain reddish-haired people with square foreheads are neither only thinkers nor only men of action, but usually . . . both." Vincent's conclusion was that Theo should renounce his business and become a painter like him.

ber of young French artists, notably Émile Bernard and Henri de Toulouse-Lautrec. Both Bernard and Toulouse-Lautrec became friendly with him and continued to admire him for the rest of their lives. Lautrec, indeed, on hearing another artist speak disparagingly of Vincent's paintings, challenged the man to a duel (fortunately forestalled).

Vincent also made the acquaintance of several other painters in the art-supply shop of a remarkable old man called Père Tanguy. Stubby, grizzled, with a look of deep kindness in his eyes—one of Vincent's portraits of him is shown on page 41—Tanguy was a former soldier who had been exiled and later pardoned for his part in the Paris Commune, the popular uprising of 1871. Though he seems to have had little education, he did have an instinctive appreciation of the new and daring in art. Because then as now this was a rare commodity, Tanguy attracted some formidably gifted men to his shop. When his customers lacked money to buy his supplies, he would trade canvas and colors for finished paintings. In time he accumulated a notable collection of works by Pissarro, Gauguin, Seurat, Guillaumin and Signac, to which a number of Vincent's paintings were soon added. For a while, Père Tanguy's cubbyhole shop was the only place in Paris where paintings by Cézanne could be seen—and purchased for as little as $20. (Cézanne apparently once met Van Gogh in Tanguy's shop, but the encounter was not a happy one—Cézanne is reported to have said, "Sir, you paint like a madman." There is no record of Vincent's reply.)

When Tanguy's artists were depressed he soothed them; when they were hungry he shared his meals with them: his shop was both a club and a gallery. He also tried to sell their paintings, in a low-keyed manner reminiscent of Theo's. An American critic wrote that the old man "had a curious way of looking down at his pictures with the fond love of a mother, and then looking up at you over his glasses, as if begging you to admire his beloved children." When Père Tanguy did find a buyer, his profit was not large. Some time after Van Gogh's death, for example, another critic wandered into the shop and saw a still life by Vincent. When he asked the price, Tanguy consulted an old ledger and said, "Forty-two francs." The critic bought the painting and inquired, "But why is it exactly forty-two, and not forty or fifty?" "Well," said Père Tanguy, "I looked up what poor Van Gogh owed me when he died. It was forty-two francs. Now I have got it back."

Although Vincent haunted Tanguy's shop, it was through Theo that he made many of his most important connections with other artists. Of these he was perhaps most impressed by Camille Pissarro. Then in his 50s, the descendant of Sephardic Jews who had been driven out of Spain by the Inquisition, Pissarro was bald and had a long white beard that gave him the look of a patriarch, which in fact he was. With Claude Monet and others, Pissarro had pioneered some 15 years before in a new style—Impressionism. It was a style about which Vincent knew almost nothing, and Pissarro, the kindest of men, was glad to explain it to him. Soon Vincent began to produce colorful, light-filled canvases that are virtually indistinguishable, at first glance, from the work of the Impressionists. It was also Pissarro, perhaps more than anyone

Archibald Hartrick, a young British painter, met most of the promising artists in Paris, including Van Gogh, whom he sketched (above). He was more impressed with the Dutchman's unpredictable behavior than with his art; he suspected that Van Gogh was a bit "cracked" and found him too quick to spout off opinions. As Van Gogh himself admitted, "I cannot always keep quiet."

in Paris save Theo, who saw Vincent's potential and sensed his tragedy. After Vincent's death he is said to have remarked that he had been sure that Van Gogh "would either go mad or leave all of us far behind. I didn't know then that he would do both."

Among other painters who thought highly of Vincent, the most intriguing is surely Toulouse-Lautrec—intriguing not so much because of his rank as an artist, although that is high enough, but because of his personality and his incandescent life. Vincent and Lautrec were very nearly as opposed in manner, mind and artistic intent as it is possible to be, yet each recognized the other's quality. Lautrec made a very perceptive portrait of Van Gogh *(page 48)*, and Vincent in turn was fascinated with Lautrec's marvelously precise line.

Toulouse-Lautrec—his full name was Henri Marie Raymond de Toulouse-Lautrec-Monfa—sprang from a vigorous, aristocratic family that could trace its ancestry back in an unbroken line to the days of Charlemagne. Counts of Toulouse, viscounts of Lautrec and Monfa, they had been closely related to the medieval kings of France. Many of them were ferocious fighters—one had been in the van of a Crusaders' assault column that cut its way into Jerusalem in 1099; another, the Marquis de Lafayette, had won fame in America. Fiercely proud, they expected their women to bear sons, not daughters—Count Alphonse de Toulouse-Lautrec, the artist's father, had once observed, before his son was born: "It is better to be a male toad than a female Christian."

The artist turned out to be a toad, possibly the ugliest man of his line, but this was not apparent in his childhood. As a young boy he was ordinary in appearance, if a trifle frail, and seemed to have only one small deficiency. His fontanel—the skin-covered aperture in the top of his skull—was an unusually long time in closing. Not until Lautrec reached puberty did it become obvious that he had a tragic ailment. He was not, as he is often called, a dwarf. He seems instead to have had a congenital weakness that affected his bones. When he was 13 he slipped on a polished floor and in the "inconsequential fall" broke his left thigh. Several months later, while he was still convalescing, he fell into a ditch and broke his right thigh. His legs never matured to normal length. At about the time of these disasters his features changed alarmingly— his nose became large and his lips gross and purplish. Later, through the use of dumbbells and a rowing machine, he was able to develop his arms and his torso—one of his friends described him as "a tiny little blacksmith wearing pince-nez"—but he could do nothing about his appearance. He was four feet eight inches tall and had only one redeeming physical asset: glowing brown intelligent eyes, into which most people were reluctant to look.

Had it not been for his incapacity Lautrec would very likely have followed his father, whom he greatly admired, into a vigorous life of hunting, horsemanship and lechery. The elder Lautrec, although he was a graduate of the French military academy, Saint-Cyr, and had served briefly in the army, was not constrained to follow an army career, and did not. The family had more than ample resources—stewards deposited the income from their estates in a large chest, from which each took whatever he needed. Lautrec's father, an eccentric on the grand scale, spent his money on hounds, hawks, horses, weapons and costumes. He often appeared in public wearing a Scot's kilt, a Caucasian helmet or the chain-mail tunic of a Crusader. Frequently he walked abroad with a falcon on his wrist; he gave his birds holy water to drink lest, as he said, they be deprived of the benefits of religion. In protest against what he claimed was the inefficiency of Parisian laundresses he once scrubbed his shirts in the gutter. When he went picnicking in the Bois de Boulogne, he did not bother to carry his food with him but instead rode a mare that had recently foaled, and milked her. On a bet he once jumped his horse over a high-roofed cab, and won. His son was lost in hero worship, but Count Alphonse unfortunately did not think much of the boy—he took it as an affront that fate had provided him with such an heir.

Young Lautrec very early revealed a keen and irreverent mind. At seven he was studying Latin and Greek. At 13 he could draw and paint animals, birds and the human figure with considerable skill. He tried landscape too, but without much success—his interest, he said, was not in nature for "nature has betrayed me." At 17, convinced that his future lay in art, he enrolled in studio classes in Paris. His father did not altogether approve of having a painter in the family; he feared it might cause gossip. Accordingly Lautrec signed his early efforts with a pseudonym, "Treclau"—an anagram of his name—or he did not sign them at all.

If Lautrec was abused or ridiculed by his fellow art students, there is no record of it. He was so vital and witty a companion that others frequently forgot his appearance—at times he even found it necessary to remind them of it. "To those who loved Lautrec," wrote one of his friends, "it required enormous effort to see him as he appeared to the rest of the world." The famous night-club singer, Yvette Guilbert, whom he sketched many times, once remarked unthinkingly as she glanced through an album of his drawings, "Really, Henri, you have a genius for distortion." At this he wheeled on her and cried, "But—naturally!" Such bitter outbursts, however, were rare.

In Paris Lautrec studied successively with two academic painters, Léon Bonnat and Fernand Cormon—the same Cormon whose classes Van Gogh also attended. By 1886, when he was 22, Lautrec had absorbed all that they could teach him, and never again bothered with formal instruction. Like Vincent he was largely self-taught, and his art cannot be pigeonholed in any school. Soon after Vincent's arrival in Paris Lautrec established himself in a studio in Montmartre, and Vincent occasionally visited him there. Another of the painters who dropped in at Lautrec's studio was Suzanne Valadon, a young lady well established in the Parisian art world. In addition to being a painter, Valadon was also a model (for Renoir, among others), a mistress (for Lautrec, among others) and a mother (at 16 she bore an illegitimate son, who later gained fame as a painter himself—Maurice Utrillo).

Suzanne Valadon left a brief account of Vincent's visits. "He arrived, carrying a heavy canvas which he stood in a corner where it got

Toulouse-Lautrec's outrageously eccentric father, Count Alphonse, once draped himself in a chain-mail helmet, tunic and dagger and strutted for the camera. The Count lived life for his own amusement and cared not at all for convention. A few days after his wedding he deserted his bride to join some old regimental cronies for a frolic in Paris. Later his only excuse was that he had completely forgotten he was on his honeymoon. At other times during their married life he impulsively left the Countess stranded on railway platforms, without a sou in her purse, perhaps to chase some young girl who caught his eye.

Like his eccentric father, Toulouse-Lautrec was fond of practical jokes and dressing up. In the photograph above he is robed in silk as a Japanese shogun, a costume he adopted for a party at the home of a rich dilettante. In the montage at top Lautrec plays a photographic prank by posing in his studio as both painter and model for a double self-portrait.

a good light and then waited for some attention to be shown. But no one bothered. He sat opposite his picture, scrutinizing the others' glances, taking little part in the conversation, and finally he left, wearied, taking his last work with him. But the next week he came back and began the same pantomime all over again." It is unlikely that Lautrec was ever deliberately rude to Vincent. The intense, humorless Dutchman was simply out of place in the gay company with which Lautrec surrounded himself, and eventually Vincent ceased his hopeful expeditions to the studio.

Lautrec, 11 years younger than Vincent, discovered alcohol at a much earlier age. "Of course one should not drink much," said Lautrec, "but often," and he would sample anything that gave him the sensation, as he put it, of "a peacock's tail in the mouth." Lautrec also discovered the world of dance halls and night clubs. Montmartre's Boulevard de Clichy and its Place Pigalle were then great centers of amateur and professional sin, affording almost every diversion known to man. If there was anything the customer wanted that was not in stock, the Montmartrois would gladly improvise it. The steep, crooked streets teemed with cutthroats and pickpockets, pimps, prostitutes, drug peddlers and homosexuals of both persuasions. Most of them had come there fairly recently. As late as 1860 Montmartre was a quiet country village on the outskirts of Paris, and even in the days of Vincent and Lautrec there were still gardens and cottages among the steaming cabarets —the Chat Noir, the Mirliton, the Divan Japonais and the Cabaret des Assassins. The ruins of a few of Montmartre's celebrated windmills also survived. One of them supplied the name for the famous dance hall that replaced it, the Moulin de la Galette (Mill of the Wheatcake). Among Vincent's paintings there are some that show Montmartre as pleasantly rural, and among the works of Lautrec some that suggest an inner circle of hell.

Lautrec was at his happiest in Montmartre at night, waddling from one cabaret to another, gesturing with the miniature cane he called a boothook, constantly spluttering, "Eh? What? Fantastic, eh? What?" He lived in a kind of democracy of deformity, accepted without question by the Montmartrois, who were too preoccupied with their own eccentricities to make an issue of anyone else's. As a rule he was accompanied by one or more companions, whom he bullied without mercy. No matter how weary they became he insisted that they stay up talking and drinking at least until dawn, sharing another bottle with him to postpone the day. At that hour Lautrec became deeply depressed and was most in need of friends.

Often Lautrec would sit for many hours in the Moulin Rouge, studying the dancers and the clientele, which ranged from low-brow to aristocratic. From time to time Edward, Prince of Wales, would turn up in Montmartre to while away an evening, and was treated like any other fat, aging bachelor. At the Moulin Rouge a dancer called La Goulue, thighs swathed in no less than 60 yards of foaming lace, knocked off his hat with a high kick, while the manager bawled, "Hullo, Wales! Is your mother buying the drinks?"

Lautrec sketched the dancers and their customers constantly, with pencil, charcoal or even a burned matchstick, trying to capture their motions and expressions with greatest economy of line. He was by instinct a caricaturist and had to struggle against it. Frequently he began by drawing one particular feature of his subject—an eye, a mouth, even a nostril —and his finished work had more exaggeration than he may have wished. One of his fellow students at Cormon's wrote that Lautrec "was always sincere in art . . . but in spite of himself he would exaggerate certain typical details, or even the general character of the figure, so that he was apt to distort without even trying or wanting to. I have known him deliberately try 'to make something pretty' of a model—even a portrait for which he was being paid—without ever, in my opinion, being able to bring it off."

Yet Lautrec seldom *intended* satire. Bitterness and mockery in his pictures are rare, and he never moralized. His intention above all was to report life as he saw it, without any of the personal involvement, the love or outrage, of Van Gogh. Lautrec, indeed, was so detached that his choice of subjects might ordinarily be found disconcerting—lesbians in bed, for example. But the grossness or weariness or disillusion in many of his pictures is no greater or less than Lautrec actually saw.

Lautrec is sometimes regarded, because of his often-reproduced posters of Montmartre entertainers, as a lighthearted or shallow artist. He was neither. His colors and designs are gay, to be sure, but he produced very little that does not provoke thought, often melancholy. As he sat in cabarets, his bowler hat pushed back on his head, he saw what most men would prefer not to see. Among the dancers who are remembered today only because of his art are Jane Avril, Grille d'Égout (Sewer Grate), Valentin le Désossé (Valentine the Boneless), La Goulue (The Glutton). It may be worthwhile to look at Lautrec's picture of the last *(page 65)* and measure it against what is known about her life and death.

Toulouse-Lautrec knew most of the great entertainers in Paris, but perhaps his favorite was the café singer Yvette Guilbert, for whom he made the oil sketch at the top. Hardly endowed with a robust figure for a chanteuse, Mlle. Guilbert nevertheless had a sharp, acid voice that pierced smoky cabarets and earned her the title "star of the end of the century."

La Goulue was only 16 when Lautrec first portrayed her. She was an Alsatian girl named Louise Weber, who seems to have been called "The Glutton" because of her habit of draining the dregs from glasses on the cabaret tables. A superb dancer, filled with animal pride, she delighted in humiliating the men who competed for her favors. But her beauty faded quickly—at 25 she could no longer find work in Montmartre, and began to tour fairgrounds in outlying cities as a sideshow. She asked Lautrec to paint a pair of panels as an advertisement, and Lautrec, loyal to his earlier friendship with her, produced (gratis) two huge canvases about nine feet square. He did not, however, confuse friendship with sentimentality. He portrayed La Goulue as almost frighteningly jaded, and in her imaginary audience he put a relentless caricature of himself and a slack-faced likeness of Oscar Wilde.

Lautrec went to see La Goulue perform in her show, and when it was over lifted his cane to her in salute and turned away. He never saw her again. Like a character in some time-condensing morality play, La Goulue descended from dancer to lady wrestler to lion tamer. With a menagerie of tired animals she toured the provinces, but went bankrupt

La Souris

L'Escargot

Le Cochon

In 1898 Toulouse-Lautrec produced 22 lithographs for a book entitled *Histoires Naturelles*, a modern bestiary written by his friend Jules Renard. Lautrec, who loved animals and was a frequent visitor at Paris zoos, did charming, sharply observed characterizations of domestic fauna, including those shown above. Renard enthusiastically exclaimed that Lautrec's pig "already makes one think of sausages!"

when one of her beasts tore off a child's arm at a fair in Rouen. She returned to Montmartre to peddle candy and flowers outside the Moulin Rouge, scene of her youthful triumphs. No doubt she hoped to be recognized by the old customers, but she was scarcely noticed. By 1925 she was a grotesquely obese and vein-faced alcoholic, trying to make a living in small-town carnivals where she billed herself as "the celebrated La Goulue." Her last employment was as a servant in a bordello. In 1929, age 59, she sensed the approach of death, called for a priest and asked him, "Father, will God forgive me? I am La Goulue."

In the year of La Goulue's passing, the French state managed to assemble and restore Lautrec's large panels for her show (La Goulue had long since sold them to a dealer who had cut them up into pieces). They were kept for a time in the Luxembourg Museum and were later transferred with reverence to the Louvre. Still later they were moved to the exquisite little Jeu de Paume, where they now hang close by the works of Lautrec's friend Vincent van Gogh.

Lautrec himself had his premonitions of death, but it is doubtful that they disturbed him. He continued to drink disastrously, calling himself a "moral suicide," but he also worked with a fury that was at least equally responsible for his early end. Relatively late in his short career he became fascinated with lithography, and at the end of a night in Montmartre he would refresh himself with a few glasses of wine in a workmen's bar, then go directly to the print shop to work. In lithography he found an art form peculiarly suited to his talents; few men have been more successful at it. The best known of his works in this field are his posters, of which he made about 30. Not all of them by any means were created for the proprietors of dance halls—he also filled orders from book publishers and manufacturers, including an enlightened American firm, which engaged him to promote the printing inks made by the Ault & Wiborg Company of Cincinnati, Ohio.

It was not unusual at the time for a fine artist to take on commercial assignments. As early as 1862, Honoré Daumier had designed a poster for a coal merchant, and in 1868 Édouard Manet had created a poster to plug a newly published book. By 1890, Jules Chéret, the most popular poster designer of the day, had been accorded two one-man shows and had received the Legion of Honor. Lautrec began by following the trend, but he soon outdistanced it. With his extraordinary control of line and his use of bold areas of flat color, he made the poster as important a form of graphic art as any other. He also gained public recognition; Parisians saw his work everywhere and were captivated by it, to the extent of peeling the posters from the walls and carrying them off for their collections. Lautrec by this time signed his own name to his work, or used his characteristic TL monogram. His father was not impressed. Upon hearing that Lautrec had many times been seen drunk in Paris, Count Alphonse asked, "Why doesn't he go to England? They scarcely notice the drunks over there."

A good many of Lautrec's works depict scenes in bordellos, and were actually made there. He often took up residence in the *maisons closes* because he was fond of their inhabitants. "The professional model," he said, "is always like a stuffed owl. These girls are alive." He shared their dinners, seated opposite the madam in a place of honor, and provided the wine and flowers. In one *maison*, on the Rue d'Amboise, Lautrec became so friendly with the madam that he decorated her salon, a fine old Louis XV room for which he painted 16 panels, each nearly six feet high, filled with garlands and girls. He was also a customer of the girls, for aside from Suzanne Valadon and one or two others who accepted him as a curiosity, no "lady" would have an affair with him. Once, when one of the prostitutes on her day off went out and bought him a bunch of violets, he was reduced almost to tears. He kept the flowers for weeks, showing them to his friends as though they were the gift of a countess.

When he was 34—it is remarkable that his health endured that long—Lautrec suffered a physical and nervous collapse. His family arranged for him to be admitted to a sanatorium in Neuilly, where he remained for several weeks. On his release he was provided with a companion, a friend who actually served as a guard to prevent Lautrec from drinking. The companion accompanied him everywhere, but with small success: Lautrec managed to get drunk whenever he pleased, and in places where no liquor was available. Eventually it was discovered that he had bought a hollow, glass-lined cane, which he filled with brandy in the morning and from which he drank whenever the guard's back was turned.

In 1901, aged 36, Lautrec left Paris and went home to die on the family estate near Bordeaux, the Château de Malromé. He was partially paralyzed, almost deaf, and suffering from a half dozen ailments. In his last hours his family sat by his bedside. His father got bored, and to break the monotony suggested that he cut off Lautrec's beard. It was, he said, an old Arab custom. Dissuaded from that, Count Alphonse contented himself with removing the elastic from his boots and snapping at flies on the counterpane. Lautrec glanced up at him and said with a smile, "The old bastard!" These were his final words. When he was buried, his father, thinking the pace of the funeral coach too slow, whipped up the horse so that the mourners walking behind were obliged to run to keep up.

Soon after Lautrec's death, one popular French critic, writing in *Le Courrier Français*, expressed an opinion that was to be shared by several others: "It is fortunate for humanity that there are few artists of his sort. Lautrec's talent, for it would be absurd to deny him one, was an immoral talent of pernicious and unfortunate influence." For more than a generation this critical hostility in the popular press continued, the burden of the complaint being that Lautrec was a wicked man, or limited in scope, or both. To the charge that he was limited in scope, it must be agreed that he found many of his subjects in the world of the dance hall, the theater and the brothel—but this is not, after all, so small a world. To the charge that his talent was "immoral," time itself has provided the reply. Those who have managed to survive the 20th Century, thus far, know by now what immorality really is—and it is not to be found in Lautrec. He is no more immoral than a mirror.

Lautrec's Demimonde

The Paris where Van Gogh painted in the late 1880s was a lightheaded city of gaiety and sin. Little of the social scene was reflected in Van Gogh's own art, but the work of another man—Henri de Toulouse-Lautrec—is a mirror of that giddy time. When Van Gogh and Lautrec met in Paris in 1886, the 32-year-old Vincent had just arrived and was barely known, even among artists. Lautrec, the son of a French aristocrat, was just 22, but had a reputation as a skilled draftsman. He was also becoming known as a wild young man who tried to forget his physical handicaps in the bawdy Parisian night life. Due to improperly healed fractures that had stunted the development of his legs, Lautrec as an adult was only four feet eight inches tall. Dwarfed and hobbled as he was—he often walked painfully with a cane and at times was pushed in a wheelchair—he nevertheless avoided self-pity. He viewed life with intellectual detachment. "I've tried simply to tell the truth, not to idealize," he once said about his art.

Lautrec plunged into the Parisian night world with abandon: he frequented dance halls, brothels and cafés, drinking copiously, talking and sketching until dawn. Attracted by people in action, he also haunted circuses, sporting events and theaters. He captured this frantic existence in paintings, drawings, engravings, watercolors and lithographs—and in the posters that made him famous. But the wild life took its toll. Like Van Gogh, he died at the age of 37, his career brilliant and brief.

Lautrec loved parties, and a joke. This lithographed invitation to a gathering at his studio in 1900 reads: "Henri de Toulouse-Lautrec will be greatly honored if you will join him for a cup of milk Saturday, May 15, at around half past three in the afternoon." Lautrec shows himself as an animal tamer with spurs and a riding crop confronting a huge cow. Milk was served at the party, but hard liquor was available in quantity from a well-stocked bar.

Henri de Toulouse-Lautrec: *Cha-U-Kao, the Female Clown,* 1899

All during his life Lautrec had a fondness for horses. Unable to ride because of his physical handicap, he still enjoyed the races, a habit cultivated by boyhood visits to tracks with his father, who was a skilled equestrian. In the lithograph at right his dynamic sense of composition and line charges horses and riders with power.

The sketch above, of a circus horse ridden by a female clown, was executed for a very specific purpose. Lautrec's health was suffering under the pressures of sleepless, drunken nights and his family was persuaded by doctor friends to commit him to a sanitarium for treatment of alcoholism. Some unfriendly critics openly rejoiced at Lautrec's confinement; to them his art had only glorified the seamy and sordid. Lautrec, for his part, felt himself imprisoned and begged to be released. Partly to prove that his drinking had not damaged his mental acuity, Lautrec completed a series of circus drawings done from memory, an arduous task since he usually worked from direct observation. The results were such triumphs that they helped the artist win his freedom.

Henri de Toulouse-Lautrec: *The Jockey*, 1899

9, Place Pigalle

P.Sescau
Photographe

Henri de Toulouse-Lautrec: *9, Place Pigalle, P. Sescau Photograph,* 1894

During the final two decades of the 19th Century, Paris fairly blossomed with bright posters and magazine covers. Chiefly responsible for this flowering of the graphic arts was the revival of lithography by artists who, like Lautrec, partly influenced by Japanese art, worked to perfect bold designs in strong colors and stark outlines. When Lautrec's vibrant posters and covers appeared on street corners and kiosks they invariably attracted attention for their striking design and their wry humor. In the advertisement above he gently caricatured a photographer, his client, at work. For the cover of a bimonthly literary review *(right)* he slyly chose as a model the wife of one of the magazine's founders. In a poster for a struggling music hall called Le Divan Japonais *(far right)*, Lautrec focused on the sensitive beauty of the then unknown dancer Jane Avril, whom he showed seated in the audience. An elderly roué, the music critic Edouard Dujardin, eyes Jane appreciatively, while the star of the show, the popular Yvette Guilbert, is shown on stage—cut off at the neck. Lautrec's clever poster could not save the music hall, which soon closed for lack of patrons. But this and other Lautrec portrayals of Jane Avril—who danced "like a delirious orchid"—helped to launch her as a star.

Henri de Toulouse-Lautrec: *La Revue Blanche,* 1895

Henri de Toulouse-Lautrec: *Le Divan Japonais*, 1892

JEU DE PAUME, MUSÉE DU LOUVRE, PARIS

Henri de Toulouse-Lautrec: *Cha-U-Kao, the Female Clown*, 1895

I n the minds of many, Lautrec is inevitably linked with one place—the Moulin Rouge. There is good reason for this: he was a regular patron of the newly built dance hall in Montmartre, and he used it as the setting of some 30 of his paintings. Lautrec understood the nature of life at the Moulin Rouge, and in his work he focused closely on its inhabitants. Above is a portrayal of the performing clown, Cha-U-Kao, who often worked there. As she adjusts her costume in a private room, the reflection of an older man, perhaps her lover, is seen in the wall mirror. In another candid portrait *(right)* the star dancer called La Goulue is seen haughtily entering the Moulin

Henri de Toulouse-Lautrec: *La Goulue Entering the Moulin Rouge*, 1892

Rouge with two other entertainers, the beefy La Môme Fromage and another, younger dancer.

La Goulue appears in action in one of Lautrec's finest paintings *(following pages)*. She is the vital focus of the scene as she does a frenzied, yet somehow elegant, dance with her long-legged partner Valentin le Désossé. In the

background at right is Lautrec's white-bearded father; at the center rear in a black cape is Jane Avril. This is Lautrec's largest painting of the Moulin Rouge, and his command is obvious: the figures are placed skillfully, the line is animated, the colors interact excitingly. Such work marked Lautrec as a first-rank artist of his time.

Henri de Toulouse-
Lautrec: *The Dance at
the Moulin Rouge*, 1890

67

LA BELLE ANGÈLE

P Gauguin 89

IV

Friends and Influences

Vincent found more stimulation in Paris than just the work of the Impressionists and Toulouse-Lautrec. The city was booming with activity, particularly in art, and Vincent did his best while there to see and assimilate all that was good among the new and the old. Before long, the bombardment of sensations, experiences and influences would prove too much for him and he would have to retreat to the countryside to work in peace. But for a while he immersed himself in Paris: he may have found a new mistress for a time; he continued his visits to Père Tanguy's shop to see what his contemporaries were up to; he came to know the important and influential young painters, including the inventor of Pointillism, Georges Seurat, and the stockbroker-turned-artist, Paul Gauguin. He was also particularly intrigued by the work of the great Japanese print makers, among them Hiroshige and Hokusai, whose brightly colored woodcuts had been imported to Europe in large numbers in recent years. Like the palette of the Impressionists, the art of Japan would greatly influence him.

It was only in 1853, the year of Vincent's birth, that Japan had been "opened" to the West by the American, Commodore Matthew Perry, who politely poked his cannon into the Japanese eye and suggested that it was time for a little commercial exchange. A few years later the first Japanese prints reached London and Paris. In 1867 and again in 1878 they appeared in the Paris world exhibitions, and were so popular that in 1883 Parisian collectors put together a show devoted exclusively to them. It was not only the picturesque subject matter—legendary figures, animals, birds, exotic costumes and landscapes—that the collectors found fascinating, but the style as well. The prints, with their flat patterns of color and lack of shadow, their strong design and decorative qualities, were unlike any then generally known in Europe. Vincent, in company with many other Western painters, happily adopted and adapted the Japanese manner himself, and often acknowledged his debt to it. In one of his finest self-portraits *(page 178)* he seems to be seeking an intensely religious feeling, but the thought of Japan was not far from his mind. As he wrote Theo, "I aimed at the character of a *bonze* [Oriental

Gauguin intended this portrait of a girl in Breton costume as a thank-you to the girl and her husband for extending him generous credit at their café. But the portrait, set like a medallion on a flower-strewn ground, did not look to them like Angèle; furthermore, Angèle's short, homely husband thought that the exotic figurine at the left was a caricature of him. The bewildered couple rejected Gauguin's gift of gratitude.

Paul Gauguin:
La Belle Angèle, 1889

69

A print by the 19th Century artist Hiroshige typifies the Japanese simplicity of style that so impressed Van Gogh and many of his fellow painters. The power of a cloudburst, for instance, is conveyed by nothing more than a series of parallel lines. Such devices were expressive of Japanese restraint; they were also partly imposed by the limitations of the wood-block medium, in which the artist's basic tool is a sharp knife. Van Gogh copied the Hiroshige print in a painting of his own (*below*), although his brush softened the boldness of the Japanese woodcut.

monk], as a simple worshiper of the Eternal Buddha. . . . I have made the eyes *slightly* slanting like the Japanese."

Although he had become acquainted with Japanese art in Antwerp, it was in Paris that he first saw the prints in large quantity—one dealer had literally a warehouse full of them. Enchanted, Vincent soon set out to form his own collection and in time accumulated several hundred items, which he valued so highly that he compared the Japanese masters—in permanence, at any rate—with the Greeks, Hals, and his countrymen Rembrandt and Vermeer.

It was the brilliant color and clear outline of the prints that most strongly caught his eye as he emerged from the dark tonalities of his Dutch period. But his constant regard for the social function of art was involved too. The prints, even after the cost of transporting them halfway around the earth, could still be sold in Paris for only one or two francs and thus were within the reach of people to whom he addressed his own work. "I do my best to paint in such a way that my work will show up to good advantage in a kitchen," he wrote, "and then I may happen to discover that it shows up well in a parlor too, but this is something I never bother my head about." He had long since sketched out an idea for an association of artists who might, through lithography, make copies of fine works of art available to workingmen at low cost, and now in Paris he approached the idea from another angle: he would arrange an exhibition of Japanese prints in a place where the general public would be likely to see it. His efforts on behalf of Japanese art were to have an unexpected effect on his own career, for in a strange way the Japanese exhibition was related to the first public showing of Vincent's paintings.

For some time Vincent had been dining in a café called Le Tambourin, not far from the apartment he shared with Theo in Montmartre. The establishment—the tables were drum-shaped and the walls hung with tambourines bearing pictures and poems contributed by the patrons—was run by an Italian woman, Agostina Segatori (*page 44*), who in her youth had served as a model for Corot. The details of Vincent's relationship with her are cloudy, but it appears that for a while she was his mistress. In any event he was able to persuade La Segatori, as she was called, to allow him to fill the restaurant with a collection of Japanese prints. There is no record of the success or failure of the show; very likely the customers paid more attention to the menu.

As his friendship with La Segatori developed, he decorated Le Tambourin with a number of his own paintings, although it is not clear whether these were hung in hopes of a sale or were gifts to the woman or commissions for which he expected to be paid. Whatever the case, the affair came to a melancholy conclusion. He got into a fight with someone in the restaurant, perhaps a waiter or customer who may have been jealous of his attentions to La Segatori, and thereafter she broke with him. In a letter to Theo, written in the summer of 1887 when Theo was on vacation in Holland, Vincent provided only hints of what had taken place. "I have been to the Tambourin, because if I did not go they would think I dared not. And I said to La Segatori that I did not judge her in this business, but that it was for her to judge herself. That

I had torn up the receipt for the pictures, but that she ought to return *everything*. That if she had not been somehow mixed up in what happened to me, she would have come to see me the next day. That since she had not come to see me, I took it that she knew they were trying to pick a fight with me, but that she had tried to warn me when she said, 'Go away,' which I did not understand at the time and perhaps didn't want to understand either. . . . I saw the waiter too when I went in, but he made himself scarce. Now, I did not want to take the pictures straight off, but I said that when you came back we could talk it over, because the pictures belonged to you as much as to me, and that meanwhile I urged her to think over what had happened again. She did not look well, and was as white as wax."

In the upshot Vincent seems not to have been able to retrieve his paintings, and later they are said to have been sold as waste canvas in bundles of 10—for as little as 10 cents a bundle. Although collectors and museum directors may grind their teeth at this, it is by no means the only instance of the wholesale destruction or disappearance of his work. In 1885, after he left Holland following his father's death, a large number of his studies were stored in a carpenter's house in the town of Breda. More than 40 years later, in 1926, a Dutch scholar visited Breda in the hope of discovering what had happened to the drawings and paintings. He found that the carpenter had given them to a junk dealer who had peddled them from a handcart. Some of them had gone to an innkeeper and he had given them as prizes to customers who consumed sufficiently large amounts of beer. Others had been used by a householder to patch holes in walls, and one had been glued as a decoration on an attic door—the door was sawed apart and delivered to restorers who removed the canvas from the wood. But of the original cache, which appears to have included more than 200 paintings, about 90 pen drawings and as many as 200 in crayon, only a fraction was recovered. Still another large hoard of early work was stored in Antwerp in 1886, just before Vincent went to Paris. No part of that priceless accumulation has ever been found.

The loss of some paintings did not discourage Vincent's attempts to display his work. In Paris he helped to organize at least two other exhibitions, with somewhat happier results than he had obtained at Le Tambourin. At one of these shows, in a huge, skylighted restaurant called La Fourche, he displayed about 100 canvases. Vincent made no sales—the customers in the restaurant, according to one observer, "tolerated the show . . . although they were a little disconcerted." However, there were indirect benefits: Vincent's circle of acquaintances among Parisian artists continued to broaden. Among those who did not exhibit, but who came to study the paintings, was Georges Seurat.

Very few great painters—perhaps only Leonardo da Vinci—have taken a more scientific approach to art than Seurat. A man of immense precision, he has the misfortune of being forever tied to an imprecise term —Pointillism—which he detested. And although he produced a number of superb works he is, in the United States, generally identified with only one of them: *Sunday Afternoon on the Island of the Grande Jatte,* the widely reproduced painting that is now the proud possession of the Art Institute of Chicago.

Seurat was 27 when Vincent encountered him, and died of an undiagnosed illness at 31, in 1891. His personal life is little known—he guarded his privacy so well that even his closest friends did not discover until after his death that he had had a mistress and a son. His artistic education was orthodox: at 18 he was admitted to the ultraconservative École des Beaux-Arts in Paris, and he studied there for about two years, concentrating on drawing and geometric theory under a teacher who was fiercely opposed to Romanticism, Impressionism or indeed any deviation from academic tradition. Outside the École, when Seurat focused his intellect on the work of his immediate predecessors—the Impressionists Pissarro, Monet and their colleagues—he found it wanting.

Seurat's objection to Impressionism was not, however, one of principle. Despite his training he strongly sympathized with the effort to create the illusion of changing natural light and color. He felt the Impressionists had not been systematic enough. In their use of quick, isolated strokes, blurred outlines and pure pigments they had ignored laws of color that Seurat believed are discoverable by science and "can be taught like music." Until his time, he thought, even the greatest masters of color had achieved their effects largely by brilliant intuition. And as it happened, Seurat's time was the right one in which to find methods and rational guidelines. The air of the late 19th Century was pervaded by science and invention; Pasteur, Darwin and Edison were household gods, at any rate among the enlightened. Seurat and his painter friends, including Paul Signac, eagerly read scientific treatises to discover what might be applied to art. Among the key works were *The Law of Simultaneous Contrast of Colors* by the Frenchman Michel-Eugène Chevreul; *Phenomena of Vision* by David Sutter, a Swiss; and *Modern Chromatics* by the American O. N. Rood, a Columbia professor.

The scientists investigated such matters as "optical mixture," which had previously been known to artists but not much used until the time of Delacroix in the mid-19th Century. Seurat now seized on this principle and made it a fundamental of his art. In order to produce green, for example, it is not necessary to blend yellow and blue pigments on a palette. The same effect, or one very near it, can be obtained by stippling many tiny, separated spots of yellow and blue on a canvas and permitting the eye to make its own mixture. To Seurat and Paul Signac, such optical mixture was preferable—it produced colors that were more vibrant and luminous. But in fact, an examination of Seurat's paintings will not support this. The colors seem muted. The "fault" lies partly in human vision, which does not respond precisely as the scientists thought it should, and partly in the paints used by Seurat, some of which had a tendency to fade. A year after his death his friend and champion, the critic Félix Fénéon, studied the *Grande Jatte* and was obliged to report: "Because of the colors which Seurat used . . . this painting of historical importance has lost its luminous charm: while the reds and blues are preserved, the Veronese greens are now olive-greenish, and the orange tones which represented light now represent nothing but holes."

However, Seurat's theories never depended on *complete* optical mixture; he was far more concerned with incomplete mixture, the effect that adjacent colors have on each other. According to a law of "simultaneous contrast of colors" set down by Chevreul, colors mutually influence one another when placed side by side, each imposing its own complementary on its neighbor. The complementary, or opposite, of blue, for example, is orange, and if the two are juxtaposed each will "reflect" upon the other, with the result that both seem strengthened and intensified. However, if noncomplementary allied colors, such as purple and blue, appear side by side, each will sap the vitality of the other.

In order to take full advantage of the simultaneous contrast of colors, without having to pause to think about "opposites," Seurat followed Chevreul's theories and constructed a color disc arranged so that complementaries were opposite each other, 180 degrees removed on the disc, and could be located at a glance. The colors that Seurat used were limited to the hues of the visible spectrum, for it was only these, the constituents of sunlight as the human eye can see it, that could, he thought, create the effect of the fleeting play of light upon the world. Black, ochers and browns, the muddy colors that exist as pigments but not as components of the sun's spectrum, were eliminated.

In painting, Seurat began by brushing in an approximation of the local color of an object—an area of green, for example, to represent a patch of turf. On this he superimposed many tiny strokes to correspond to the influence of the colors of nearby objects. But then, since he was dealing not only with color but with light itself, he added other strokes (dots) to indicate direct light and still others for reflected light. The many strokes were optically mixed by the viewer, and the fragmentation of color and light on the canvas gave rise to the term by which the style was known to Seurat—Divisionism. The popular term, Pointillism, refers more to a stippling technique than to Seurat's theory.

It is true that Seurat frequently used the tip of his brush to make small round dots, but these were only incidental to his system. Any small strokes resulting in dashes, ovals or commas would have served as well, and all these can in fact be found on his canvases—which were never executed in a drearily uniform, mechanical way. For his pains, Seurat was obliged to endure ferocious criticism from critics, laymen and fellow artists—his technique was called *"petit-point,"* pregnant women were facetiously warned not to look at his pictures lest their children be born speckled, and Paul Gauguin is said to have called him "a little chemist." However, Seurat had the self-confidence to accept this with a shrug.

The critic Fénéon, almost alone, grasped what was in progress, and in Seurat's lifetime set down this description: "If you consider a few square inches of uniform tone in Monsieur Seurat's *Grande Jatte*, you will find on each inch of its surface, in a whirling host of tiny spots, all the elements which make up the tone. Take this grass plot in the shadow: most of the strokes render the local value of the grass; others, orange-tinted and thinly scattered, express the scarcely felt action of the sun; bits of purple introduce the complement to green; a cyanic blue,

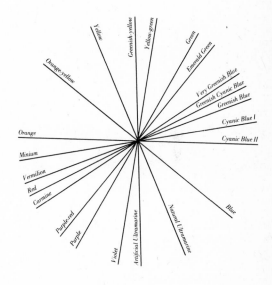

To help him select precisely complementary colors, Seurat copied a diagram like the one above from a textbook by the American physicist and amateur painter Ogden N. Rood. The wheel identifies 22 exact complementaries, using the names of artist's pigments rather than scientific terms. Rood's book also discussed the optical phenomenon by which dots of pure color, seen at a distance, tend to blend into new, mixed colors in the human eye. This became a basis for Seurat's Pointillist brush technique.

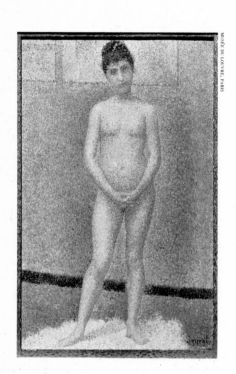

The evenly sized dots of paint that Seurat so often used in his Divisionist technique are apparent in the nude study above. By using separately colored points of paint, a method derived from scientific principles of color mixing, Seurat believed he more closely matched the effects produced by colors in nature. But he also preferred the technique because it made vibrant colors and allowed each bit of paint to dry evenly, thus assuring consistent tones throughout a painting.

provoked by the proximity of [another] plot of grass in the sunlight, accumulates its siftings toward the line of demarcation, and beyond that point progressively rarefies them. Only two elements come together to produce the grass in the sun: green and orange-tinted light, any interaction [of reflected light or complementaries] being impossible in the furious heat of the sun's rays."

Fénéon, to distinguish between the "old-fashioned" or "romantic" Impressionists in one category, and Seurat and his friends (Paul Signac particularly) in another, first used the term Neo-Impressionists for the latter, who are sometimes called Scientific Impressionists as well. The distinction between the two sorts of Impressionists is easily made—with one exception. Camille Pissarro, that admirable, open-minded man, produced work of both kinds. Having been one of the originators of Impressionism in his youth, Pissarro in his mid-fifties recognized the brilliance of Seurat's theories and made a number of Divisionist pictures. But Pissarro soon abandoned Divisionism, not because he considered it unsound but because he was temperamentally unsuited to it. He preferred reasonably quick results and could not bring himself to spend two years on a single canvas, as Seurat had done on the *Grande Jatte*. He continued to paint until his death at 73, despite a painful eye ailment and a respiratory problem that caused Theo van Gogh to note that the old fellow was "wearing some kind of muzzle."

Seurat persisted in his methodical approach for the duration of his brief career. But it was not only Divisionism with which he was concerned. He was also engrossed with an attempt to recapture the calm dignity and monumentality of early Italian Renaissance masters, particularly Piero della Francesca. His figures, almost always presented in front, back or profile view, are so logically and precisely placed that it would seem to require dynamite to move them.

Seurat also had a sharply defined theory of esthetics, based partially on old truths long known by intuition to painters and partially on modern research in psychology. In brief summary, Seurat held that a sense of calm and order in painting is obtained by a balance of light and dark tones, of cool and warm colors, and by establishing an equilibrium between horizontal and vertical forms. Gaiety results from a dominance of light or luminous tones, warm colors and lines that seem to spring upward; sadness by the opposites. These ideas, to be sure, seem commonplace and not thunderous today, but it was Seurat who made the formal statement of them and it was he who first applied them rigorously. In his work absolutely nothing was left to chance or to the first impression. All his forms are carefully simplified, so that even the most bourgeois subjects acquire a new grandeur and dignity—a formidable and perhaps antiseptic art, but one that has had great impact on the work of the 20th Century.

Vincent's emotional approach to art was at the opposite pole from Seurat's, but Vincent understood and admired him. With Theo he called on Seurat in his studio, where the *Grande Jatte* hung on the wall near work still in progress. For a time in Paris Vincent made Divisionist pictures of his own, although he was inclined to use the small strokes more for their textural value than otherwise. His instinct was toward plowed fields of paint and toward thick impasto—both impossible in Seurat's canon. What he most appreciated in Seurat was his work with complementary colors—in discussions of art Vincent would frequently shout "Blue . . . orange! Blue . . . orange!" In his later paintings he used complementaries with more effect than any painter before or since, with perhaps the sole exception of Matisse.

Vincent probably learned Seurat's theories not from the artist himself but from Signac, who was Seurat's friend and the man most responsible for articulating his theories. An intelligent and gay companion, Signac befriended Vincent and accompanied him on painting expeditions to Asnières, a suburb of Paris on the Seine. On such occasions Vincent often carried a very large canvas which he would divide into several rectangles in order to make a number of studies at one session—"a little museum," as one acquaintance called it. (The divided canvases have all vanished.) In Signac's recollection, "Van Gogh, dressed in a blue plumber's blouse, had painted little dots of color on his sleeves. Close beside me he shouted and gesticulated, brandishing his large, freshly covered canvas, and with it he smeared himself and passersby with all the colors of the rainbow."

Vincent's enthusiasm was almost always beyond control. Archibald Hartrick, the Briton who described him as "glancing back at you over his shoulder and hissing through his teeth," had somewhat more to say about his eccentric behavior while in Paris. Hartrick shared a flat with another English artist, Henry Ryland, who was rather a feeble type—he was prone to sick headaches and produced "weak watercolors of the 'La belle dame sans merci' type." On one occasion Vincent dropped in to pay a call on Hartrick but found only Ryland at home. Seeing the watercolors, Vincent launched into a furious diatribe on the nature of true art. When Hartrick returned he found Ryland "a sickly yellow," his head wrapped in a towel soaked in vinegar. "Where have you been?" cried Ryland. "That terrible man has been here for two hours waiting for you and I can't stand it any more."

Vincent recognized his own shortcomings. "I cannot always keep quiet," he said, "as my convictions are so much a part of myself that it is sometimes as if they took me by the throat . . . [but] it always hurts me, it makes me nervous, when I meet somebody about whose work I have to say, 'But that is neither good nor bad, that really does not look like anything,' and it gives me a sort of choking feeling that stays with me, till some day I find out he has something good in him."

Vincent occasionally disconcerted both strangers and acquaintances by his mere appearance. A few of the self-portraits he made in Paris *(pages 178-179)* reveal him as well-dressed, almost natty, but as a rule he was not—he preferred to be taken for a laborer. That is how he was described by Paul Gauguin, the one great painter who knew him intimately and who left behind observations of him that were sharply detailed if not always objective. In a book of memoirs called *Avant et Après* Gauguin saw not only the appearance but also the character of the man:

"It is beginning to snow. It is winter. You get a shroud gratis: that is what the sheet of snow is. The poor freeze, though the landlords often cannot grasp this. Walking more rapidly than usual, and without any desire to go out and make merry, pedestrians on this December day bustle along in the Rue Lepic in our good city of Paris. Among them is one man who is shivering with cold and is dressed in a queer manner. He is hurrying along, down the outer boulevards. He is wrapped in a goatskin and wears a fur cap, probably rabbitskin, and has a straggly red beard. A cattle drover would look like that.

"Don't glance at him superficially, don't go on, despite the cold, without observing his well-shaped white hand, his childishly clear blue eyes. He must be a poor devil.

"His name is Vincent van Gogh.

"He hurries into a shop where they sell old ironwork, arrows of savages and cheap oil paintings.

"Poor artist! You gave away part of your soul when you painted the picture which you are now trying to dispose of.

"It is a little still life: pink shrimps on pink paper.

" 'Can you let me have a little money for this picture, so I can pay my rent?'

" 'Mon Dieu, my friend, my trade is getting difficult too. They ask me for cheap Millets! Then, you know,' adds the shopkeeper, 'your painting is not very gay. The Renaissance is the thing nowadays. Well, they say you have a talent and I should like to do something for you. Here is five francs.'

"And the coin chinks on the counter. Van Gogh takes it without protest, thanks the shopkeeper and goes. He goes up the Rue Lepic again with a heavy tread. Near his lodgings a wretched streetwalker who has just escaped from the St. Lazare comes along, smiling at him, hoping for a client. Van Gogh is well read. He thinks of La Fille Elisa [a then-current novel about a prostitute], and his five-franc coin belongs to the poor creature. He dashes off, as though ashamed of his generosity, with an empty stomach."

There is one detail in Gauguin's anecdote that seems unlikely—Vincent would scarcely have been concerned about paying the rent while living in Theo's apartment—but otherwise it has the ring of truth. Gauguin, like Vincent, was a prolific writer. The two painters were also alike in that both had come very late to art, and both were belligerently positive in their ideas—but here the similarity ended. Gauguin, muscular and self-assured, was as hardheaded in his beliefs as Vincent was idealistic; there was almost nothing on which the two men could agree for more than a few days. Nevertheless they entered into a strange friendship, which in Vincent's case was touched with hero worship. Although Gauguin was only five years older than he, Vincent looked up to him as a superior man and artist, and for a time would gladly have become his disciple.

Vincent first met Gauguin in Paris in November 1886—he had earlier seen several of Gauguin's pictures in the Impressionist show of that year, where Seurat's Grande Jatte was also hung. A commanding and almost theatrical figure, Gauguin wore a beret pushed low over his

Mette Gauguin gathered her five children about her for a formal portrait in Copenhagen in 1888. It had been five years since her husband had forsaken finance for art, and four since they tried to hold their marriage together by moving to Mette's home in Copenhagen. There Gauguin had tried to paint while working as a traveling salesman, but by June 1885 he was determined to make a complete break and returned to Paris, leaving Mette in Denmark. He visited Mette and the children briefly before he left for Tahiti in 1891 (when the photo below was taken), but they never lived together again.

eyes, walked with a rolling gait and carried a walking stick that he had carved with bizarre designs. His background was exotic, and he frequently used it to impress others. Born in Paris, he had passed part of his boyhood in Lima—his mother was of Spanish-Peruvian stock, and it was his boast that he had the blood of the Inca in his veins. As a youth he had served in the French merchant marine, had sailed around the world, and in the Franco-Prussian War had been a crewman aboard a corvette in the North Sea. But at 23 he had turned to a business career and had taken a job as a stockbroker in the Paris Bourse. For 11 years he had worked there, sometimes earning the handsome annual income of 40,000 francs. He had married a proper Danish girl from Copenhagen, fathered four children, and had shown every sign of settling into a comfortable bourgeois middle age. But at 34 he had quit the Bourse and informed his disapproving wife that he intended to become a painter.

Although the change did not come without warning, Gauguin's wife never forgave him for it—she had bargained for a well-to-do businessman and took it as domestic treason when he turned to art and suddenly had no income at all. In his moneyed days he had begun to paint as a Sunday pastime and had also invested fairly heavily in what his wife considered trash—works by Cézanne, Manet, Renoir, Monet, Pissarro and others. As a collector he had met Pissarro, who undertook to instruct him in painting, and from that time onward his interest in the Bourse rapidly waned. By his 31st year, in 1879, he had become so skilled as an "amateur" that his work (with Pissarro's sponsorship) was exhibited in the fourth show arranged by the Impressionists, and he continued to display his pictures with them until the eighth and last show in 1886—by which time his business career was over.

When Vincent met him Gauguin's savings were gone—in the preceding winter, close to starvation, he had worked as a billposter in a freezing Paris railroad station at five francs a day. His wife and children (there were now five) had moved to Copenhagen to live near her mother, taking the family furniture with them—when Gauguin implored her to send him a few blankets she allowed him to shiver for two months before complying. However, there was nothing in the least hangdog about Gauguin; he was a supreme egotist who expounded his theories of art with a vehemence that amounted to rudeness, quarreling with his old friend Pissarro and then with Seurat, whose ideas he had at first admired. He talked constantly of voyaging to the tropics, which he knew at first hand, and where he believed the roots of art could be rediscovered in pure atmosphere, brilliant colors and societies still uncorrupt. A few months after meeting Vincent, Gauguin proved to be as good as his word—he took ship for the island of Taboga, off the Isthmus of Panama, where "the air is very healthy, and for food, there are fish and fruit for nothing." His act cannot have failed to impress Vincent, who admired men who followed their art wherever it led, and who already had some awesome credentials in that regard himself.

Gauguin's fond vision of a painter's paradise was very soon shattered. Taboga had become "civilized" since he had visited it as a merchant seaman. An international company headed by the French engineer Ferdinand de Lesseps, who had supervised the construction of the Suez Canal, was attempting to duplicate the feat in Panama. Some 10,000 laborers were sweating among the snakes and rats in the mosquito-infested swamps; a rest home for them had been built on Gauguin's island. Prices of food and shelter were outrageous and the local police vicious, harrying any stranger who seemed to them a vagrant. Gauguin was obliged to work as a laborer on the canal, swinging a pick for more than 12 hours a day to earn passage money to another island, Martinique, where he hoped conditions might be better. But when he got there he was dogged by sickness and poverty; he auctioned off his watch at dockside and went to live in a hut by the edge of the sea. Yet somehow he managed to paint, and after a seven-month absence made his way back to France with several canvases.

Gauguin's paintings had, or hinted at, a kind of mystery, a suggestion of thoughts a trifle too deep for words, and they impressed Vincent van Gogh when he saw them exhibited at Theo's gallery. Possibly the paintings impressed him overmuch; perhaps he read his own profound meanings into what was merely decorative. In any case he would have occasion to see Paul Gauguin at deadly close range soon enough.

It was time for Vincent to leave Paris and, like Gauguin, strike out again on his own. He had had more than enough stimulation—Japanese art, the Impressionists, Seurat and Signac, Lautrec and Gauguin. His own work had already changed greatly—he no longer tried primarily to express his love for mankind by depicting men, particularly the poor and oppressed, but sought to state it in landscapes and still lifes, offering his feelings on a less direct but more complex level. In Paris he had found that it was not necessary or perhaps even desirable to make a picture of a poor peasant in worn-out boots in order to make his point. Instead he painted only the boots themselves; and these in their rugged shabbiness conveyed far more. Nor did he need to work in hues of tarnished coins and green soap—brilliant color spoke more powerfully and more directly.

As his art had changed, so had his relations with those around him. Nervous and exhausted, he had begun to drink heavily and to quarrel with Theo. In desperation Theo wrote to their youngest sister, Wilhelmina, at home with their mother in Holland:

"My home life is almost unbearable; no one wants to come to see me any more because it always ends in quarrels; besides, he is so untidy that the place looks far from attractive. I wish he would go and live by himself; he sometimes speaks about it, but if I were to tell him to go away, it would be just a reason for him to stay. Since I can do nothing right for him, I only ask for one thing: that he does not cause me any trouble. But by staying with me he is doing just that, for I can hardly bear it.

"It is as if he had two persons in him—one marvelously gifted, delicate and tender, the other egotistical and hardhearted. They present themselves in turn, so that one hears him talk first in one way, then in the other, and this always with arguments which are now all for, now all against the same point. It is a pity that he is his own enemy, for he makes life hard not only for others but for himself."

But when Wilhelmina advised Theo to "leave Vincent for God's sake," Theo replied, "It is such a peculiar case. If he only had another profession, I would long ago have done what you advise me. I have often asked myself if I have not been wrong in helping him continually, and have often been on the point of leaving him to his own devices . . . but I think in this case I must continue in the same way. He is certainly an artist, and if what he makes now is not always beautiful, it will certainly be of use to him later; then his work will perhaps be sublime."

Without pressure from Theo, Vincent reached his own decision. He knew that he was on the verge of a complete breakdown, sodden with alcohol and unable to control his nerves. To save himself he would have to leave Paris. In February 1888 he suddenly departed for southern France, intending to go first to Arles and then to Marseilles. He had heard much of the Midi from Toulouse-Lautrec, who in his youth had spent some time there, and he was attracted by the prospect of a warmer sun and brighter sky. Indeed, although there is no great resemblance between southern France and Japan, he had convinced himself that the two were very similar. As he told Theo, "We like Japanese painting, we have felt its influence—all the Impressionists have that in common—then why not go to Japan, that is to say to the equivalent of Japan, the Midi? Thus I think that after all the future of the new art now lies in the south."

It was impossible for bitterness to exist between the brothers for very long. Before departing, Vincent arranged his room in Theo's apartment so that Theo might have the feeling he was still there—he decorated the walls with Japanese prints and left one of his paintings on the easel. He took the train to Arles, and after he had gone Theo wrote once more to their sister: "It seems strange to be without him. He meant so much to me."

Gauguin: A Late Beginning

Paul Gauguin, the 35-year-old French stockbroker who suddenly abandoned the position, luxuries and responsibilities of a middle-class businessman to devote his life to painting, has become a sort of folk hero to every desk-bound dreamer. His amazing decision, however, was neither so abrupt nor so reckless as it might seem. Gauguin certainly lived richly, affording himself a brougham with driver, denying his wife no fashionable extravagance, carpeting his home with Oriental rugs, stocking his garden with rare roses. But there was another side to his life. He had painted as an amateur for many years. He chose a house in a Paris suburb where artists lived; he covered its walls with contemporary paintings, and worked long hours in a huge studio in the garden. After leaving his office, he haunted the many art galleries near the Stock Exchange, and studied at a variety of art schools before he became a pupil of the Impressionist master Camille Pissarro. Some of his pictures had been exhibited and admired, and he optimistically assumed that he could maintain his scale of living by painting. He was mistaken. Less than three years after he gave up his regular job in 1883, everything was gone—including his wife, who took his five children, furniture and art collection to her native Denmark. In 1886, with money borrowed from a friend, Gauguin left Paris to live at a cheap village inn in Brittany. It was there, during the next four years, that his distinctive style slowly emerged.

One of the strongest influences on Gauguin's developing style was that of Japanese prints, also admired by such other artistic innovators as Cézanne and Van Gogh. Typically Japanese devices in this tabletop still life are the arbitrary perspective, the flat planes, the uniform areas of color, and bold outlines around the puppies, bowls, fruit and glasses.

Paul Gauguin: *Still Life with Three Puppies*, 1888

les misérables

Paul Gauguin: *Self-Portrait (Les Misérables)*, 1888

Paul Gauguin: *Portrait of Meyer de Haan*, 1889

In Brittany Gauguin found an unexpected premium: the companionship of sympathetic artists. A few other painters, like Van Gogh, whom he met in Paris in 1886, had admired his work, but here a whole group of young artists was attracted to him. He became especially fond of Émile Bernard, who described the new style that Gauguin envisioned in such erudite phrases as "the idea is the form of things outside those things." Though Gauguin reveled in this high-flown talk, he was better with paint than with words, and he worked like a man possessed. In a self-portrait *(left)*, painted as a gift to his friend Van Gogh, he inset a profile of Bernard on a flat background studded with posies —symbols of innocence. An inscription that Gauguin wrote on the work, *les misérables,* refers not only to the proverbial poverty of artists, but to their common bondage in a lifelong quest for perfection. Here Gauguin was "synthesizing" an essential reality—the likenesses are abstracted but brilliantly characteristic of the men and they are subtly combined with symbolic ideas. Similarly, the portrait study above of the dwarfed painter Meyer de Haan includes such overt symbols as the lamp of truth, books of poetry and philosophy, and the apples of Eden.

83

Paul Gauguin: *The Gate*, 1889

Paul Gauguin: *Brittany Landscape with Swineherd*, 1888

Brittany's harsh, spare landscape turned out to be the perfect place for Gauguin to find himself. "When my wooden shoes ring on this granite," he wrote, "I hear the muffled, dull, powerful tone I seek in my painting." During several sojourns there from 1888 to 1890, he gradually dropped the lyric realism of his Impressionist mentors. In *Brittany Landscape with Swineherd (above)*, the beginnings of this break with his previous style can be read clearly from left to right: at left, particularly in the bright flowering shrubs, he used exactly the kind of brushwork Camille Pissarro had taught him. But the bold, flat planes of the rounded hills fading away to the right—suggestive of Japanese art—show his newly emerging style. Struggling for a graphic expression of the theories his more vocal friends talked out, he tried to "synthesize" the simple forms of Brittany's small, boulder-strewn farms with the idea of dreary toil. Convinced that every artist has a moral responsibility to his God-given talent—that he must work hard because he has been gifted—Gauguin also felt a warm sympathy for these other "miserables," the Breton peasants who tilled a rocky soil. In *The Gate (left)*, he may have sought to express this identification with the poor farmers in a personal symbolism. Gauguin was forever coming and going—from Paris and Brittany, to Arles, to Tahiti—and the roughhewn gate may have represented to him, as it might for an ambitious Breton peasant, both the closing of an old way and the opening of a new road to freedom.

85

Paul Gauguin: *Vision after the Sermon (Jacob Wrestling with the Angel)*, 18

Gauguin was fascinated by the Breton women. Their plain dark dresses and stiffly starched white collars, caps and aprons seemed to fall into picturesque patterns whatever they were doing. But more than their appearance it was their simple, almost archaic piety that inspired him. In some of his finest works of the period he combined them in typical local scenes with the great themes of religious drama. In a picture of Jacob wrestling the angel *(above)*, Gauguin shows a cluster of prayerful Breton women dressed in their Sunday best. Evidently they have just come from church—their priest stands at the right—and they are transfixed by a vision from the Old Testament, perhaps the subject of the morning sermon. Painted in flat, boldly outlined, contrasting colors, the picture reveals how keenly Gauguin understood the power of superstition and imagination over the Breton peasants' minds. And he chose his colors both for their pictorial impact and for their symbolic overtones. The dominant red tonality—powerful in itself —around the distant vision may realistically represent the daybreak in which Jacob recognized his heavenly foe, or it may symbolize the field of spiritual battle.

Symbol and reality also blend beautifully in *The Yellow Christ (right)*, in which Gauguin reached a peak of expression. Peasant women in workaday clothes—one wears a sackcloth apron—kneel by an outdoor crucifix; or is it perhaps the Crucifixion itself? Gauguin's moving portrayal of the women's devotion makes the symbolic scene seem as real as if it were happening at that very moment. The culmination of his experience in Brittany, this picture foreshadows, both in technique and theme, the great South Sea Island works that would follow.

86

Paul Gauguin: *The Yellow Christ*, 1889

V

The Southern Sun of Arles

Van Gogh's palette, already lightened by his stay in Paris, blooms with the beauty of a southern spring in a painting done a few months after his arrival in Arles. The artist was at work on this study when he received word of the death of a cousin, the Dutch painter Anton Mauve. Vincent immediately dedicated the painting to Mauve's memory.

Peach Trees in Blossom "*Souvenir de Mauve*," April 1888

The small city of Arles stands beside the Rhône River about 55 miles inland from the Mediterranean. Arles is very old—Julius Caesar and Constantine sojourned there, and maintained it as one of the key centers of communication in the Roman Empire. Roundabout there are many ancient works in stone: monuments, tombs, theaters, aqueducts; and beside them are relics of medieval times when Arles was the capital of a kingdom. Scattered among them lie other stones only recently hewn, flat, without inscription, little more than a square foot in size, set in the pavement of the winding streets. They mark the spots where Vincent made his paintings, and were placed in 1962 in celebration of a "Van Gogh Year." Difficult to locate, polished by the tread of passersby who scarcely notice them, they will last as long as any Roman stones, commemorating a man who did not seek to seize or hold a kingdom but to give one away.

Another artist might have been intrigued by the antiquities of Arles, but Vincent had no desire to paint them. He was a man of his own time; even when his mind ranged far afield it journeyed into the future, not the past. "There is a Gothic portico here," he wrote to Theo soon after he had left Paris for this town in the south of France, "which I am beginning to think admirable, the porch of St. Trophime. But it is so cruel, so monstrous, like a Chinese nightmare, that even this beautiful example of so grand a style seems to me to belong to another world, and I am as glad that I do not belong to it as to that other world, magnificent as it was, of the Roman Nero."

It was the light and color of Arles that overwhelmed Vincent, the blossoming fruit trees, the oleanders, the violet earth, the olives and cypresses. In his letters the word "Japan," which to him was almost a synonym for color, sounds over and over like an incantation. He wrote of "a meadow full of very yellow buttercups, a ditch with irises, green leaves and purple flowers, the town in the background, some gray willows, and a strip of blue sky. . . . A little town surrounded by fields all covered with yellow and purple flowers; exactly—can't you see it?—like a Japanese dream." Although the distance from Paris to Arles is only about 450 miles, he had indeed traveled to a far country, and it was here that his art reached its zenith. Enchanted and driven by the sun with its "high, yellow note," he became convinced that a new manner of painting was to be born in southern France, and that "the painter of the future will be a colorist such as has never existed."

There have been many analyses of Vincent's explosion of color in Arles—both of his methods and his intent—but the most interesting is his own. He did not expect to be immediately understood, even by so knowledgeable a man as Theo, and thus his letters are filled with many scattered, fragmentary explanations. In his portraits, for example, he had begun to depart radically from conventional colorism even before coming to Arles. In part, this was his reason:

"I should like to paint the portrait of an artist friend, a man who dreams great dreams, who works as a nightingale sings, because it is his nature. He'll be a blond man. I want to put my appreciation, the love I have for him, into the picture. So I paint him as he is, as faithfully as I can, to begin with.

"But the picture is not yet finished. To finish it I am now going to be the arbitrary colorist. I exaggerate the fairness of the hair, I even get to orange tones, chromes and pale citron-yellow.

"Behind the head, instead of painting the ordinary wall of the mean room, I paint infinity, a plain background of the richest, most intense blue I can contrive, and by this simple combination of the bright head against the rich blue background I get a mysterious effect, like a star in the depths of an azure sky."

Referring to his just-completed portrait of a peasant, Vincent continued: "Again in the portrait of the peasant I worked this way, but in this case without wishing to produce the mysterious brightness of a pale star in the infinite. Instead, I imagine the man I have to paint, tormented in the furnace heat at the height of harvest time, as surrounded by the whole Midi. Hence the orange colors flashing like lightning, vivid as a red-hot iron, and hence the luminous tones of old gold in the shadows. Oh, my dear boy . . . and the good people will only see the exaggeration as caricature."

It was not only in portraiture that Vincent's color burst forth. The still lifes and the landscapes of Arles blaze with it as well. Nor was it only in a handful of pictures. In the year 1888 his production was torrential. Between his arrival in February and his hospitalization after his mental collapse in December he made at least 90 drawings and 100 paintings, among them many that are now world-famous: *The Drawbridge, Old Peasant, Sunflowers, The Zouave, Starry Night on the Rhône, Fishing Boats on the Beach at Saintes-Maries, The Arlésienne.*

The volume of his output became almost an embarrassment. Vincent felt obliged to justify himself to Theo, who received the paintings by freight in Paris and apparently sent back remarks critical of his speed from men in the profession. Vincent defended himself by referring to the speed of Claude Monet, who had recently produced 10 canvases in four months: "Quick work doesn't mean less serious work, it depends on one's self-confidence and experience. In the same way Jules Guérard, the lion hunter, says in his book that in the beginning young lions have a lot of trouble killing a horse or an ox, but that old lions kill with a single blow of the paw or a well-placed bite, and that they are amazingly sure at the job."

In a following letter he spoke of the natural flow and ebb of creativity. "I must warn you that everyone will think I work too fast. Don't you believe a word of it. Is it not emotion, the sincerity of one's feeling for nature, that drives us? And if the emotions are sometimes so strong that one works without knowing one works, when sometimes the strokes come with a continuity and a coherence like words in a speech or a letter, then one must remember that it has not always been so, and that in time to come there will be hard days, empty of inspiration. So one must strike while the iron is hot, and put the forged bars on one side."

The quantity and quality of Vincent's work are remarkable enough, but appear even more impressive in view of the conditions in which he worked. In one of his first letters from Arles he reported that "I have been for several walks in the country hereabouts but it is quite impossible to do anything in this wind. The sky is a hard blue with a great bright sun which has melted almost all the snow, but the wind is so cold and dry that it gives you goose flesh." This was his first encounter with the mistral, the violent and sometimes terrible wind that blows south down the valley of the Rhône to the Mediterranean. Later he wrote of the valley, "What a picture I would make of it, if there was not this damned wind. That is the maddening thing here, no matter where you set up your easel. And that is largely why the painted studies are not so finished as the drawings; the canvas is shaking all the time." He drove pegs into the ground and tied the legs of his easel to them; sometimes he was forced to lay his canvas flat on the earth and paint on his knees. In the end he came to think of the wind as an enemy that had defeated him, and spoke sadly of what he might have been able to do if the mistral had permitted it.

His health was as precarious as ever. In a state of near-collapse when he came to Arles, he recovered briefly but soon began to work at a suicidal pace, describing himself as "a painting engine." Haunted by his debt to Theo, he wrote: "Today again from seven o'clock in the morning till six in the evening I worked without stirring except to take some food a step or two away. . . . I have no thought of fatigue, I shall do another picture this very night, and I shall bring it off." For one three-week period he subsisted on only bread, milk and a few eggs, yet reported that "I even work at midday, in full sunlight, with no shade at all, in the cornfields, and enjoy it all like a cicada." Occasionally he indicated that he realized how close he was to collapse, but made no complaint. In fact he began, with unconscious irony, to give advice to Theo, who had recently been ill: "Go to bed *very early*, because you must have sleep, and as for food, plenty of fresh vegetables, and no *bad* wine or *bad* alcohol. And very little of women, and *lots of patience*."

The people of Arles, although he wrote warmly of them, did not reciprocate his affection. His appearance and habits alarmed them. When he arrived in town he walked from the railroad station to a small hotel nearby, and was admitted somewhat grudgingly by the innkeeper. Soon there were quarrels—it was charged that Vincent, with all his equipment, took up more space than the other guests and should pay extra. (Ultimately he was obliged to go to a justice of the peace to obtain the release of some of his belongings, which the innkeeper had seized.) When he went abroad to work, "always very dusty, always more bristlingly loaded, like a porcupine, with maulsticks, painter's easel, canvases and further merchandise," he was not viewed as an adornment to the town. What was worse, he seemed obsessed with painting the stars, and could be seen working at night—when the mistral was not blowing—with his hatband stuck full of lighted candles for illumination.

But Vincent was tolerated at first, and managed to persuade several of the Arlésien townspeople and peasants to pose for him, although he found that they were disappointed when they saw "nothing but paint on the canvas." Among those who were willing to accept immortality from him, only one, the local postman, Joseph Roulin *(page 106)*, became his close friend. Roulin not only posed six times himself but offered his family as sitters as well: his wife, his two young sons and a newborn daughter.

Vincent also struck up an acquaintance with a colorfully uniformed lieutenant of Zouaves, P. Milliet, who was on leave in Arles after having fought in Indochina. The portrait of Milliet *(page 107)* is very widely known; less so is what the painter and model had to say of each other. Lieutenant Milliet took some drawing lessons from Vincent, and later recalled that the artist was "a strange fellow, impulsive like someone who has lived a long time in the sun of the desert. . . . A charming companion when he knew what he wanted, which did not happen every day. We would frequently take beautiful walks through the countryside around Arles and out there both of us made a great many sketches. Sometimes he put his easel up and began to smear away with paints. And that, well, that was no good. This fellow who had a great taste and talent for drawing became abnormal as soon as he touched a brush. . . . He painted too broadly, paid no attention to details, did not draw first. . . . He replaced drawing by colors."

Vincent complained wistfully that the lieutenant was so lecherous that he made an unreliable model. "He poses badly, or I may be at fault myself, which, however, I do not believe, as I am sorely in want of some studies of him, for he is a good-looking boy, very easy-going and unconcerned in his behavior, and would suit me damned well for the picture of a lover. . . . He hardly has any time to spare, seeing that he must take a tender leave of all the whores and tarts in the tart-shops of Arles, now that he has to return to his garrison, as he says. I do not object to it, but I regret that he has a nervous motion of the legs when posing. He is a good fellow, but he is only twenty-five, God damn it."

Milliet's objection to Vincent's technique as a painter was not an unreasonable one for a layman to have made in 1888. No doubt it shocked Milliet that Vincent had ceased to bother with making preliminary charcoal sketches on his canvases, but worked directly in color. He drew with his brushes, applying his paint in strokes that formed his contours, and had no need of underdrawings. In his eagerness "to exaggerate the essential, and purposely leave the obvious things vague," he worked with dazzling haste and remarked that he had "no system at all. I hit the canvas with irregular touches of the brush, which I leave as they are. Patches of thickly laid-on color, spots of canvas left uncovered, here and there with portions that are left absolutely unfinished, repetitions, savageries. . . . Working directly on the spot all the time, I try to grasp what is essential in the drawing—later I fill in the spaces that are bounded by contours—either expressed or not, but in any case *felt*— with tones that are also simplified, by which I mean that all that is going to be soil will share the same violet-like tone, that the whole sky will have a blue tint."

To "fill in the spaces," the great flat planes of color that appear in so many of his paintings, Vincent used brushwork that amounts to a personal signature: broad strokes interwoven in a lattice pattern, or in successive "halos" around a head, a lamp or the sun. Far from having "no system at all," he developed a style so distinctive that even a layman can recognize his unsigned canvases almost as readily as those bearing his name.

Again and again his letters from Arles return to the subject of color. In writing of *The Night Café (pages 114-115)*, he noted that "I have tried to express the terrible passions of humanity by means of red and green. The room is blood red and dark yellow with a green billiard table in the middle; there are four citron-yellow lamps with a glow of orange and green. Everywhere there is a clash and a contrast of the most disparate reds and greens in the figures of the little sleeping hooligans, in the empty, dreary room. . . . I have tried to express the idea that the café is a place where one can ruin oneself, go mad or commit a crime."

Yet *The Night Café*, for all the sense of horror that Vincent set forth in it, is affectionate in its intent: an admonition or warning, not an indictment. He repeatedly spoke of his purpose in using strong color, which was the same one that had long ago inspired him to enter the ministry "to give hope to poor creatures." It was his belief that "it is actually one's duty to paint the rich and magnificent aspects of nature. We are in need of gaiety and happiness, of hope and love. The more ugly, old, vicious, ill, poor I get, the more I want to take my revenge by producing a brilliant color, well-arranged, resplendent." He spoke of wanting "to say something comforting, as music is comforting," and of his longing to "express hope by some star, the eagerness of a soul by a sunset radiance . . . isn't it something that actually exists?" In making his portrait of Madame Roulin, the postman's wife, he portrayed her holding the handle of an unseen cradle, for he imagined the painting hung in the cabin of a fishing boat, to comfort storm-tossed sailors with reminders of their childhood. The thought was a naïve one—but Vincent was a naïve and extremely vulnerable man who could have been shattered by anyone with the wit and the cruelty to do it.

When he had been in Arles a few months he moved from his hotel to a small house nearby that he was able to rent for 15 francs a month—although it had two stories the house contained only four rooms, and the

lavatory was next door. He was very proud of the place: "My house here is painted the yellow color of fresh butter on the outside with glaringly green shutters; it stands in the full sunlight in a square which has a green garden with plane trees, oleanders and acacias. And it is completely whitewashed inside, and the floor is made of red tiles. And over it there is the intensely blue sky. In this I can live and breathe, meditate and paint."

"The yellow house" was far more than a home and a studio for Vincent. Its very color, his favorite above all others, was symbolic. He soon began to see it as "the house of light," a place where the new "school of the South" might be founded. Reviving his earlier hopes of an artists' commune, he imagined that other artists might come to live with him, and that they might share their expenses and profits. He thought of Paul Gauguin, of Georges Seurat and Émile Bernard, one of the young painters who had befriended him in Paris. "My dear comrade Bernard," he wrote, "more and more it seems to me that the pictures which must be made, so that painting should be wholly itself, and should be raised to a height equivalent to the serene summits which the Greek sculptors, the German musicians, the writers of French novels reached, are beyond the powers of an isolated individual; so they will probably be created by groups of men combining to execute an idea held in common.

"One may have a superb orchestration of colors but lack ideas. Another is cram-full of new concepts, tragically sad or charming, but does not know how to express them. . . . All the more reason to regret the lack of a corporative spirit among artists, who criticize and persecute each other, fortunately without succeeding in annihilating each other."

In letter after letter Vincent expounded his hopes to Theo, and increasingly the hopes became centered on Paul Gauguin. At that time

Van Gogh's home in Arles—seen in his watercolor painting on the opposite page and in the photograph at left—was a modest two-story structure that housed a grocery store in addition to Vincent's small apartment. Using a few hundred francs Theo had sent him, Vincent was able to make the place habitable within a few months after he arrived in 1888. He called it his "yellow house"—a name symbolic in Japanese culture of a "house of friendship"—because he had high hopes for the impending arrival of his friend Gauguin. Sometime after Van Gogh's death in 1890, the ground floor of the building was converted into a bar, which it remained until it was bombed out in 1944.

Gauguin was painting in Brittany, ill and impoverished. Could not Theo arrange it so that Gauguin could come to Arles, perhaps by giving him a monthly allowance too? In his enthusiasm Vincent saw his society of artists already established, and wrote that "as there will now be several painters living together, I think we shall need an abbot to keep order, and naturally it is going to be Gauguin."

Vincent eagerly proceeded to furnish his yellow house, imploring Theo for extra money to buy beds, chests, sheets and a kitchen range— "Gauguin has been a sailor; he can cook very well." It was also important to Vincent to decorate the house with the finest paintings he could produce—"Well, yes, I am ashamed of it, but I am vain enough to want to make a certain impression on Gauguin with my work, so I cannot help wanting to do as much as possible alone before he comes. His coming will alter my manner of painting and I shall gain by it, I believe, but all the same I am rather keen on my decorations, which are almost like French painted porcelain." He covered the walls of Gauguin's bedroom with magnificent pictures of gardens. And he filled his own room with dazzling sunflower paintings, having gone hungry so that he could buy frames for them.

Yet when the idea was proposed to Gauguin, he delayed. He was, he claimed, too sick and too deeply in debt to make the trip. Vincent, however awed he may have been by "my friend Gauguin," sensed that there was a vein of craftiness in him and told Theo that "I feel instinctively that [he] is a schemer who, seeing himself at the bottom of the social ladder, wants to regain a position by means which will certainly be honest, but at the same time, very politic. Gauguin knows little that I am able to take all this into account." However, he soon wrote Gauguin a self-abasing letter—"I always think my artistic conceptions extremely ordinary when compared to yours. I have always had the coarse inclinations of a beast. . . . [But] I think that if, from now on, you begin to feel like the head of a studio, which we shall try to turn into a refuge for many . . . [we can be] full of courage with regard to the success of our enterprise, and you must go on considering this your home, for I am very much inclined to believe that it will last long. A cordial handshake."

In October 1888, Theo bought 300 francs' worth of Gauguin's pottery. He also agreed to pay Gauguin a monthly stipend in return for future paintings, and later that month Gauguin set out for Arles. Vincent was apprehensive, fearful that his little house and his preparations might seem inadequate to so sophisticated a man. "Maybe you will be disappointed in Arles, if you arrive at a time when there is a mistral, but wait. . . . It is only after some time that the poetry of this place grips one. You will not yet find the house as comfortable as we shall try to make it, little by little. There are so many expenses!"

In the last letter he wrote to Theo before Gauguin's arrival, Vincent spoke for the first time in Arles of "madness," adding that "I must beware of my nerves." For a man who wished to "express hope by some star," and who was about to be confronted by another man who would tell him that "Arles is the filthiest place in the Midi," that was something of an understatement.

Gauguin had nothing to say about Vincent's beloved yellow house itself; it was the general untidiness that struck him. "Between two such beings as he and I, the one a perfect volcano, the other boiling inwardly too, a sort of struggle was preparing. In the first place, everywhere and in everything I found a disorder that shocked me. His color-box could never contain all those tubes, crowded together and never closed."

Gauguin very early saw "that our common finances were taking on the same appearance of disorder," and undertook to set up a budget, allowing for food, rent, tobacco and "hygienic excursions" to the brothels at night. He also remarked that their modest treasury was replenished "by his brother, a clerk at Goupil's." It is surprising that he should have called Theo a clerk; certainly Gauguin must have known better. Mistakes of that sort flaw his account. And there are larger errors. Gauguin reported that when he arrived in Arles he found Vincent "floundering . . . with all his yellows and violets, all this work with complementaries—a disorderly work on his part—he only achieved soft, incomplete and monotonous harmonies; the sound of the trumpet was lacking. I undertook the task of explaining things to him, which was easy for me, for I found a rich and fruitful ground. . . . From that day Van Gogh made astonishing progress; he seemed to become aware of all that was in him, and thence came all of the series of sunflowers after sunflowers in brilliant sunshine." The sunflowers, of course, were already framed on the wall when Gauguin turned up.

However, the two artists were by no means estranged during the first weeks; indeed they never lost their regard for each other, even after their association was melodramatically severed after Vincent's collapse. They painted together (although they did not choose the same motifs) in a vineyard, in the public garden and in the Alyscamps (Elysian

Fields), an avenue of Roman tombs. Gauguin did not share Vincent's hope of founding a "school of the South"—he talked instead of going to the tropics in a year—nor did he admire the surroundings that so enchanted Vincent. "I find everything small, paltry, the landscape and the people," he wrote. But from Vincent's side, at least, matters seemed to be going well. As he told Theo, "He is a very great artist and a very excellent friend."

In the evenings they discussed art theory, in which Vincent was more than willing to take lessons. Although his instinct was to work directly from life, he allowed himself to be persuaded by Gauguin that "abstractions" were superior. "I am going to set myself to work from memory often," he told Theo, "as the canvases from memory are always less awkward, and have a more artistic look than studies from nature." As it developed, Vincent was unable to do this, and afterward confessed that abstraction was "an enchanted territory, old man, and one quickly finds oneself up against a wall."

Their conversations about portraiture also came to a dead end—"Gauguin and I talked about this and other analogous questions until our nerves were so strained there wasn't a spark of vital warmth left in us." Earlier, Vincent had written of their discussions: "Our arguments are terribly *electric*, sometimes we come out of them with our heads as exhausted as a used electric battery."

By early December the tension between the two men had become intolerable. Gauguin wished to leave Arles; Vincent was well aware of it. All his hopes for the "school of the South" doubtless seemed in ruins and he began to behave strangely—although there is only one firsthand account of his actions: Gauguin's. And that account must be assessed by the reader in the light of the inaccuracies that have been found elsewhere in Gauguin's recollection.

According to Gauguin, "During the latter days of my stay, Vincent

Gauguin's portrait of Van Gogh, done in Arles in 1888, shows the painter concentrating at his easel. During that time Van Gogh was working on a series of portraits of the people of Arles, but somehow he never attempted to paint one of his housemate, Gauguin. Perhaps he felt intimidated by the older man, or perhaps Gauguin simply lacked the patience to sit for him. In any case, Van Gogh did paint a "portrait" of Gauguin's chair *(page 111)*—his "empty place" as Van Gogh called it.

would become excessively rough and noisy, and then silent. On several nights I surprised him in the act of getting up and coming over to my bed. To what can I attribute my awakening just at that moment?

"At all events, it was enough for me to say to him, quite sternly, 'What's the matter with you, Vincent?' for him to go back to bed without a word and fall into a heavy sleep.

"The idea occurred to me to do his portrait while he was painting the still-life he loved so much—some flowers. When the portrait was finished, he said to me, 'It is certainly I, but it's I gone mad.' " (In a letter to Theo written months later, Vincent used somewhat different language: "Have you seen the portrait that he did of me, painting some sunflowers? Afterward my face got much more animated, but it was really me, very tired and charged with electricity as I was then.")

In Gauguin's account, "That very evening we went to the café. He took a light absinthe. Suddenly he flung the glass and its contents at my head. I avoided the blow and, taking him bodily in my arms, went out of the café across the Place Victor Hugo. Not many minutes later Vincent found himself in bed where, in a few seconds, he was asleep, not to awaken again till morning.

"When he awoke, he said to me very calmly, 'My dear Gauguin, I have a vague memory that I offended you last evening.'

"Answer: 'I forgive you gladly and with all my heart, but yesterday's scene might occur again, and if I were struck I might lose control of myself and give you a choking. So permit me to write to your brother and tell him that I am coming back.'

"My God, what a day!"

Gauguin did write to Theo, saying that he could not continue living with Vincent "because of incompatibility of temper." But in a following letter he took it back, referring to the first as "a bad dream." For several days the two remained in the yellow house. On December 23rd Vincent sent a note to his brother: "I think Gauguin was a little out of sorts with the good town of Arles, the little yellow house where we work, and especially with me. As a matter of fact, there are bound to be grave difficulties to overcome here too, for him as well as for me. But these difficulties are more within ourselves than outside. Altogether I think that he will definitely go, or else definitely stay. . . . I am waiting for him to make a decision with absolute serenity."

It is not easy to visualize Vincent as serene in such circumstances. Gauguin certainly was not. Later he wrote to a friend: "Ever since the question arose of my leaving Arles he had been so queer that I hardly breathed any more. He even said to me: 'You are going to leave,' and when I said 'Yes,' he tore a sentence from a newspaper and put it into my hand: '*The murderer has fled.*' "

On Christmas Eve, according to Gauguin, "I had bolted my dinner, I felt I must go out alone and take the air along some paths that were bordered by flowering laurel. I had almost crossed the Place Victor Hugo when I heard behind me a well-known step, short, quick, irregular. I turned about on the instant as Vincent rushed toward me, an open razor in his hand. My look at that moment must have had great power in it, for he stopped and, lowering his head, set off running towards home.

"Was I negligent on this occasion? Should I have disarmed him and tried to calm him? I have often questioned my conscience about this, but I have never found anything to reproach myself with. Let him who will fling the stone at me.

"With one bound I was in a good Arlésien hotel, where, after I had inquired the time, I engaged a room and went to bed."

After this encounter, which occurred a day earlier than Gauguin recalled, Vincent returned to the yellow house and slashed his left ear with the razor. It would seem to be of small importance whether he cut off the entire ear or only the lobe, but the affair is so bizarre that scholars argue about it, producing such studies as "*Vincent van Gogh et le drame de l'oreille coupée*" in the French medical journal *Aesculape*. According to Theo van Gogh's widow, who was surely in a position to know, only the lobe was removed.

When Vincent had stopped the flow of blood, he put on a large beret and carried the severed portion of his ear wrapped in newspaper to a nearby brothel that he and Gauguin had frequented. According to a brief news item in the Arles paper of the time, "Last Sunday night at half past eleven a painter named Vincent van Gogh, a native of Holland, appeared at the *maison de tolérance* No. 1, asked for a girl called Rachel, and handed her his ear with these words: 'Keep this object like a treasure.' Then he disappeared. The police, informed of these events, which could only be the work of an unfortunate madman, looked the next morning for this individual, whom they found in bed with scarcely a sign of life."

The gift of the ear lobe had caused an uproar in the streets, but Gauguin had slept through it. The next morning, as he recalled it, he went to the yellow house and was accosted by a policeman who "said to me abruptly and in a tone that was more than severe, 'What have you done to your comrade, Monsieur?'

"'I don't know. . . .'

"'Oh, yes . . . you know very well. He is dead.'

"I could never wish anyone such a moment, and it took me a long time to get my wits together and control the beating of my heart. Anger, indignation, grief, as well as shame at all these glances that were tearing my person to pieces, suffocated me, and I answered stammeringly: 'All right, Monsieur, let us go upstairs. We can explain ourselves there.'

"In the bed lay Vincent, rolled up in the sheets, all in a ball; he seemed lifeless. Gently, very gently, I touched the body, the heat of which showed that it was still alive. For me it was as if I had suddenly got back all my energy, all my spirit.

"Then in a low voice I said to the police superintendent: 'Be kind enough, Monsieur, to awaken this man with great care, and if he asks for me, tell him that I have left for Paris. The sight of me might prove fatal to him.'"

Gauguin left the yellow house. Vincent was taken to the hospital. It seemed doubtful that he would live, and in the opinion of most of the townsfolk it scarcely mattered.

A Sunburst of Painting

The brilliant light of southern France flooded into Van Gogh's life—and art—at Arles. "Those who don't believe in this sun here are real infidels," he wrote his brother Theo in August 1888. He had arrived in Arles from Paris in February, just before the almond trees burst into bloom and spring flowers began to blossom. After the grays of his native Holland and the muted colors of Paris, Van Gogh was stunned with pleasure at the sight of the colorful countryside. The fields were alive with the green of growing crops, the azure skies were deep and wide, and the magnificent sun caused the land to glow and vibrate with rich and subtle hues.

Van Gogh wrote his friend the painter Émile Bernard, "In the south, one's senses get keener, one's hand becomes more agile, one's eye more alert, one's brain clearer." He was understating the case. During his 15-month stay at Arles, Van Gogh worked feverishly in one of the most prolific and inspired bursts of artistic creativity ever recorded. From February 1888 to May 1889, he produced some 200 paintings, as well as scores of drawings. Many of these canvases are undisputed masterpieces; all reflect light, color, energy. This immense outpouring, however, exacted a monstrous toll; Van Gogh had driven himself to a limit of emotional and physical exhaustion that left him spent. His work under the sun at Arles established him as a giant in art, but when it was over he had only one year left to live.

The sun of Arles, which so influenced the art of Van Gogh, dominates the countryside in this detail from *The Sower (following page)*. Using a heavily loaded brush that left each touch distinct, Van Gogh filled the sky with brilliant colors.

The Sower, June 1888, detail

The Sower, June

In Arles, Van Gogh pursued his stated belief that "color expresses something in itself." To achieve this end, he began to make an almost arbitrary use of color, and sought the exact harmonies that would "express the love of two lovers by a wedding of two complementary colors, their mingling and their opposition, the mysterious vibrations of kindred tones." He strove for these electric juxtapositions while painting everyday scenes of the south.

One of the artist's best-known works, *Sunflowers (right)* conveys the warmth of color Vincent found at Arles. He made many of these sunflower studies as decorations for his rooms, and each radiates his passion for light, color and simplicity. *The Harvest (following pages)* is also a comparatively tranquil painting, a subtle blend of lush green and yellow fields offset by violet shadows on the sides of the wagons, houses and hillsides. By contrast, *The Sower (above)* pits the powerful violet of a freshly plowed field against the bright yellows of standing wheat and a sun-filled sky. The sower himself seems a bridge between these strong colors; his body blends with the field while his eyes are at the level of the yellow horizon. The short, almost harsh, brush strokes heighten the tensions created by the colors.

102

Sunflowers, August 1888

The Harvest,
June 1888

The Postman Roulin, August 188

Portrait of Lieutenant Milliet, September 1888

F ew Arlésiens would sit for portraits by Van Gogh; they distrusted the intense stranger from the north. Some did befriend him, however, among them the postman Joseph Roulin *(left)*. A solid citizen, posed in full uniform, Roulin was an engaging man. This manner is transmitted by his expression; his eyebrows are raised as though he was constantly startled, yet amused, by the world around him. Another friend was Lieutenant P. Milliet *(above)*, whom Van Gogh painted with honest simplicity. His regimental crest is set in the solid background, and his pale complexion is heightened by pink ears and lips, which complement his scarlet cap.

Bedroom at Arles,
October 1888

The Chair and the Pipe (also called *Van Gogh's Chair*), December 1888-January 1889

In the south, Van Gogh was a desperately lonely man. Many of his paintings, like the picture of his bedroom on the preceding pages, reflect his yearning for companionship. He wrote his brother Theo, "The sight of this picture is meant to relax the mind, or rather the imagination." The painting is indeed relaxing, yet the subtle signs of his loneliness appear in the way the solitary artist longingly paired every object: two pillows, two chairs. Even the pictures hang in pairs.

The arrival in Arles of his friend Gauguin late in October 1888 should have ended Van Gogh's lonely days. But the strong personalities of the two artists clashed

VINCENT VAN GOGH FOUNDATION, AMSTERDAM

Gauguin's Chair, December 1888-January 1889

constantly, producing tensions and arguments that finally forced Gauguin to leave. Earlier, Van Gogh had begun studies of the chairs the two men customarily used *(above)*, works that, completed after Gauguin's departure, seem to be portraits of the men themselves. Gauguin's chair, seen by candlelight, is a sophisticated design with armrests and curved legs. The upright, lighted candle placed next to two books generates a robust, active aura. Van Gogh's chair, by comparison, is bathed in sunlight, its workmanship rough and simple. Standing alone, with the artist's unlit pipe and tobacco pouch on its seat, it speaks eloquently of his desolation.

Café Terrace at Night, September 1888

Van Gogh worked throughout the broiling Arles summer, painting under the sun. Then, instead of resting, he often set up his easel outdoors at night and painted until dawn, using candles stuck in his hat to provide him with light. Van Gogh enjoyed the hours after dark. "The night is more alive, more richly colored than the day," he once wrote. In several oils, including *Café Terrace at Night (above, detail left)*, he caught the easy conviviality of the southern summer evenings. The lantern of the café glows hospitably; townspeople sip drinks, chat and stroll under the stars, which hang like lamps in the royal-blue sky.

But the night harbored demons, too, ones that the artist understood. In *The Night Café (following pages)*, he explored the terrors of the night's underworld in strident colors. "I have tried to express the terrible passions of humanity by means of red and green," he explained in a letter to Theo. Indeed, the colors seem to mix like acids, combining to create lethal fumes. Drunken patrons slump at their tables; overhead the lamps are circled by jagged halos, and the painting's perspective lures the viewer's eyes toward a bright yellow doorway—a hint of other nighttime enticements. Van Gogh himself knew well the temptations of the bars and brothels of Arles. What he could not know was that he was on the verge of a complete mental breakdown.

113

The Night Café,
September 1888

114

IA ORANA MARIA

VI

Gauguin in Paradise

It is often suggested that the cynical, sarcastic Paul Gauguin goaded Vincent van Gogh to the breaking point in Arles. Certainly Gauguin did Vincent no good, but it is unfair to charge him with malice. Gauguin was so complete an egotist that he was seldom aware of the damage he inflicted on those around him, too preoccupied with his own problems to offer much kindness to others. When the two men came together to share the yellow "house of light" in the south of France, a clash was inevitable, and in the nature of things it was Vincent who would suffer while Gauguin walked away unscathed. He regarded Vincent's tragedy as a nasty personal inconvenience, and soon was back in Paris hoping to raise money for another voyage to the tropics.

The vague outline of Gauguin's life is well known in the Western world; it is one of the legends that help to make humdrum existence more bearable. To a society smothering in obligations Gauguin symbolizes escape of the most delicious kind: to the gentle air of the South Seas, far beyond commuting and computing, where delicacies need only be plucked from the trees and shared with precocious girls who, as Gauguin said, "invade one's bed." Moreover, Gauguin's myth permits duty-haunted desk-bound man to have his cake, or breadfruit, and eat it too. It is important to be successful, not merely a beachcomber, and did not Gauguin on occasional effortless afternoons produce masterpieces that are worth a fortune?

Gauguin's myth is public property. If he were now alive he would scarcely be permitted to change it. Rather than hear him say that his life in the South Seas had not always been idyllic, most pale office workers would prefer to throttle him. Indeed Gauguin was made aware of the importance of his myth, as opposed to the relative triviality of his human existence, during his lifetime. When he was prematurely old, diseased and desperate on the island of Hiva Oa in the Marquesas, he wrote to one of his few friends in France and expressed the wish to come home. The friend replied, in effect: For heaven's sake, don't do it. You are already held in the esteem accorded to the famous dead; why spoil everything? Gauguin remained in Hiva Oa and died there.

Gauguin's Varied Sculpture

Shortly after his marriage, Gauguin, still only a Parisian Sunday painter, acquired a landlord who was also a sculptor. Taking up this art, Gauguin produced a few orthodox portrait busts, like the one of his son below. Later he threw off convention and produced a revealing self-portrait in the form of a stoneware mug—a head with eyes shut and ears omitted, suggesting an artist who relied on inner visions and voices. Gauguin subsequently incorporated this mug, sprouting flowers, in one of his still-life paintings. His later sculpture *(opposite page)* was usually exotic, reflecting his life in the tropics, even when—as in the case of the wooden barrel—he actually carved it in France.

Bust of his son Émil

Self-portrait mug

Paul Gauguin, whatever the popular belief may be, was not a happy man. He felt victimized by a callous world that did not understand him, as it has failed to understand other great men. It did not occur to him that the world may have understood him rather well, and merely returned the casual cruelty and indifference that radiated from him. His artistic genius, however, seems beyond dispute—as he was among the first to acknowledge: "I am a great artist and I know it. It is because I am that I have endured such sufferings." Extremely vigorous and versatile, he worked in oil, watercolor, pastel, pencil and ink. He made multicolored woodcuts as well as etchings and lithographs. When a furnace was available to him he produced ceramics. He made at least one portrait bust in marble and a number of bas-reliefs in wood. If no better material was at hand, he carved the trunks of trees. He sketched and painted on windows, walls and doors, and while he was wearing the local costume of Brittany he decorated even his wooden shoes.

One of the most active "borrowers" in all art, Gauguin took ideas from a score of sources, often lifting them intact with little pretense of alteration—the wrestling figures in *The Vision after the Sermon* on page 86, for example, were transposed from a print by the Japanese master Hokusai. Elsewhere in Gauguin's work there are copies of motifs from Egyptian and Greek sculpture, from the primitive art of Latin America and Polynesia, and from many Western artists, including Botticelli, Delacroix, Millet, Degas, Courbet, Daumier, Manet, Prud'hon and the school of Rembrandt. At times Gauguin was content to take an ordinary snapshot or a newspaper illustration and press it into service.

As to whether Gauguin was a master plagiarist, however, the reply is surely No. His borrowings were combined with his own artistic visions, and his completed works have an originality that is beyond serious question. Although it is sometimes startling to recognize a familiar motif in one of his paintings, invariably the motif has been subordinated to Gauguin's purpose.

At the time of his sudden departure from Arles in December 1888, leaving Van Gogh in the hospital, Gauguin was in his 41st year and still developing his art. Having begun as a follower of the Impressionists, he was now in strong reaction against them, rejecting their attempts to capture the fleeting effects of light and atmosphere in favor of sharply outlined figures and areas of flat unmodulated color. Although he had had more luck than Van Gogh, in that he had sold at least a few paintings, he had not been able even to give away his best work to date, the *Vision*. When he offered it to a Breton church the priest found it so "crude" that he thought it probably was a hoax and declined it.

In May 1889 Gauguin managed to display a number of his paintings at the Paris world's fair—full of optimism, he dragged them to the fair himself in a handcart. He was not of course invited to hang them in the official pavilion, where only "recognized" artists were given space. His exhibition hall was a café close by the newly built Eiffel Tower on the fairgrounds. One of Gauguin's friends persuaded the owner to permit him to decorate the walls. The persuasion was not difficult—the café proprietor had ordered a shipment of mirrors from the great factory at Saint-

Gobain, and when these were not delivered in time it became necessary to fill the blank space with something, even modern art. Gauguin, through Theo, invited Vincent to contribute a few canvases—Gauguin thought that six might be an appropriate number, while he himself exhibited 10. Theo, however, on his brother's behalf, quickly turned down the offer, not because of the discrepancy in the number of paintings but because he felt that exhibiting in the café would be undignified, "like entering the world's fair by the back stairs."

Gauguin's venture was a financial fiasco. Not a single painting was sold. Patrons came to the café in large numbers, but primarily to gape at an orchestra of 12 lady violinists accompanied by a lone male cornet player and conducted by an alleged Russian princess. Critics did arrive, but one noted, "It is not easy to approach these canvases on account of the sideboards, beer pumps, tables and the bosom of the cashier." To the popular eye the great sensation of the fair was not art but the Eiffel Tower itself, although painters, who were heard to refer to it as "the junkman's Notre Dame," generally ignored it. Among major artists only Georges Seurat made a study of it.

In matters other than sales, however, Gauguin's show was far from a failure. Young artists and writers, who had seen only random samples of his work or had merely heard reports of his ideas and personality, had an opportunity to study a representative selection and were deeply impressed by the paintings and by the painter himself. Gauguin, although he was only five feet four inches tall, had such presence that he seemed to take possession of whatever room he entered, driving others into the corners. He had, according to a French poet who observed him at the time, "a narrow brow and a nose more broken than curved or hooked, a mouth with thin straight lips, and heavy eyebrows which would slowly rise to reveal a pair of slightly protruding eyeballs with bluish pupils that rotated alternately to left and right, while he never troubled to allow his head or body to keep company with them."

Gauguin's conversation about art was formidable, although he had little education and lacked Van Gogh's wide background in reading. "I am two things which can never be held up to ridicule," he once remarked, "a child and a savage." It was his wish "to liberate painting from the shackles of probability." The attempt to imitate the colors of nature was a waste of time; colors came from tubes. "How do you see those trees?" he asked. "They are yellow. Very well, put down yellow. And that shadow is rather blue. So render it with pure ultramarine. Those red leaves? Use vermilion." It was necessary to reduce forms to their basic outlines, to avoid shadows, and to scorn modeling in light and shade—it was in that area, he said, that inferior artists were prone to cheat. He felt that "there is no such thing as *exaggerated art*. I even believe that there is salvation only in the extreme." However, his work was in no sense primitive. He began with the complicated, and systematically reduced or synthesized it, striving to rediscover the mysteries that can be glimpsed if one goes "beyond the horses of the Parthenon to the wooden horses that children play with." In his ideas lie many of the sources of 20th Century art.

Moon goddess, votive girl (back to back)
COLLECTION ALDEN BROOKS

Carved and painted barrel
MARLBOROUGH-GERSON GALLERY, NEW YORK

Stoneware cup with bathing girl
COLLECTION MRS. ESTHER BREDHOLT, COPENHAGEN

A picturesque photograph *(top)*, taken by a French businessman who lived in Papeete, provided Gauguin with the subject and composition for a watercolor *(center)* and a bas-relief *(bottom)*, as well as for a painting. Gauguin titled them all *Pape Moe*, or *Mysterious Water*, and related them to a legend of a princess who was startled while drinking at a waterfall and, in her fright, swam into a hole leading to the underworld.

Gauguin's theories were particularly congenial to the French Symbolist poets who came into prominence late in the 1880s. In the Symbolist view the old academic realism in poetry and painting was outworn and had never come to firm grips with life in the first place. The real truths lay in dreams, memories, phantoms and hallucinations. (This, to be sure, was also the opinion of Sigmund Freud, who at that time was developing his theories of psychoanalysis in Vienna.) In literature and art it was necessary to express ideas by new means—by veiled hints and allusions, effects of strangeness that convey not the mere appearance of an object or situation but what the artist *feels* about it. It was time, in the phrase of the French novelist J.-K. Huysmans, to "substitute the dream of reality for reality itself."

When Gauguin expressed such ideas as "art is an abstraction. Seek it in nature by dreaming in the presence of it . . ." he seemed a sort of 19th Century soul brother to the Symbolist writers, who adopted him. He had long expounded his thesis that the primordial, secret roots of truth could be found in the tropics, where dusky Eves and Adams still survived in their own Edens. The Symbolists were not committed to the notion that the tropics were the only place to look—there were some interesting Adams, Eves and deep dreams in Montmartre as well—but felt obliged to assist a man whose ideas were kindred to theirs. So they set out to help Gauguin raise money for a voyage to Tahiti.

Gauguin's principal champion was the literary critic and poet Charles Morice, who used the power of the press to promote a great sale of Gauguin's paintings in Paris. Morice badgered the editors of avant-garde magazines and newspapers for favorable publicity, and persuaded the immensely popular writer Octave Mirbeau to produce a laudatory article for *Écho de Paris*. Gauguin himself was not inactive; he twisted the arm of everyone who could help him, and in doing so annoyed his onetime teacher and friend Camille Pissarro. Distressed by the brouhaha that Gauguin was creating, Pissarro protested against anyone who would "get himself elected a genius." Auguste Renoir was scarcely happier, pointing out that "one can paint as well in the Batignolles," a district of Paris, as in some exotic location. Paul Cézanne is said to have accused Gauguin of having stolen an artistic concept of his "in order to roam with it through the South Seas."

The sale was a remarkable success, largely because of the drum-beating in the press but also because Gauguin's romantic, sardonic personality was much talked about. He exhibited 30 paintings done in Martinique, Brittany and Arles and sold all but one of them, realizing at least 7,500 francs (about $1,500) after expenses for catalogues, framing and commissions. As a side benefit he was able to obtain a letter of "official mission" from the government, an honor that entailed no salary but entitled him to a 30 per cent reduction in his steamship fare and to be treated with respect by officials in the colonies.

Before his departure for Tahiti, Gauguin went to Copenhagen to see his family. He had long since been separated from them; six years had elapsed since he had seen his children, who now ranged in age from seven to 16. When he had been able to spare the money he had sent them small sums, and apparently he still hoped for a reconciliation in the vague future—in a letter at about this time he greeted his wife, Mette, as "My adored Mette." She, who had been living on the benevolence of her friends and her earnings as a translator of French into Danish, seems also to have retained some sparks of affection but was prudent. With five children, she did not relish the possibility of a sixth and insisted that Gauguin sleep not in her home but in a hotel.

The visit cannot have been very pleasant. Mette's family despised Gauguin. The children had been brought up to speak only Danish, which Gauguin had never learned well, and he was saddened to discover that most of them could scarcely say more in French than "*Bonjour, mon père.*" Only one, his 13-year-old daughter, Aline, who had been christened in honor of Gauguin's mother, established any rapport with him. She appeared to understand his total commitment to art and to sense the unhappiness in him, and solemnly told him that "later on I shall be your wife."

Gauguin probably did not share the proceeds of his sale with his family. Mette was not in actual want nor was she, despite his occasional protestations of love, invariably charming. She sometimes spoke of him as "that monster" and referred to "these children, whom, God knows, I never wanted." She appears to have been an attractive woman but was fond of wearing men's clothes and of smoking cigars. One of the last records of her, after Gauguin's death, places her in a compartment reserved for women on a French train. The conductor, seeing what he assumed to be a cravat-wearing, cheroot-puffing male in the wrong place, demanded instant departure and discovered that he was talking to Mette Gauguin.

The artist's journey to Tahiti via Suez was lengthy but uneventful. He arrived in Papeete, the capital, in June 1891, bearing his paints, 100 yards of canvas, a shotgun (for securing food when the breadfruit failed), a French horn, a guitar and two mandolins, the better to thrive in a love- and music-making society. He was disillusioned very soon. The culture of Tahiti, like that of almost all remote islands that—in the dreadful but accurate pun of anthropologists—have been syphilized by the West, was somewhat decayed. Gauguin already had syphilis, having contracted it in Paris, but still expected to find noble savages; he was 100 years too late. Two weeks after his arrival the last native King of Tahiti, Pomaré V, died—much to Gauguin's sorrow, for he had counted on the idea that a local savage would help a European savage such as himself. The King, who had no power and was only tolerated by the French authorities, had drunk himself to death at 52. The King's father, grandfather and great-grandfather had also perished in the same way. Gauguin attended the royal funeral. Pomaré V was laid to rest in a stone mausoleum 15 feet high, painted red and surmounted by what had been intended to be a Grecian urn but actually resembled a huge liquor bottle.

Although Gauguin's letter of "official mission" secured him an audience with the French governor and dinner invitations from the elite of the European community, which then numbered about 300, there were also drawbacks. The governor, who could scarcely believe that Gauguin had come some 11,600 miles from Paris merely to paint pictures, assumed that he was a spy sent to snoop on the colonial administration. Gauguin, for his part, found the governor and the other Europeans distressingly mediocre, inferior to the degraded native Tahitians. Soon he left Papeete and made his way 30 miles along the coast to the district of Mataiea, where he rented a hut and commenced to paint.

The natives in Mataiea had suffered somewhat less from civilization than had those in Papeete, but the district had felt its impact far more than Gauguin indicated in his art. There was a primary school operated by French nuns and a general store run by a Chinese merchant. Several of the houses were made of planks and tin, and there was a patrolling gendarme. Gauguin soon discovered that the problem of obtaining food was by no means easy. Food *was* available on the mountainsides and in the lagoons, but it required an athletic, knowledgeable native to gather it. The task would have occupied most of his waking hours. The natives also had garden plots, but Gauguin knew nothing of Tahitian agriculture. He could not buy food from his neighbors because they considered such traffic undignified, nor could he ask them for it—his European pride stood in the way. The Chinese merchant sold food, to be sure, but did not deal in fruit, eggs, vegetables, fresh pork or fish because there was no market for them. Everyone, except Gauguin, had all he needed. Thus Gauguin found himself, on the island of plenty, in the ironic situation of living almost entirely on canned foods, macaroni and dried beans, for which he paid dearly because they were imported delicacies.

These unexpected expenses, plus the cost of rent, tobacco, wine and absinthe, which he consumed in large quantities, placed great strain on Gauguin's purse. However, he had left a number of paintings in the hands of friends and dealers in Paris, and expected that these would soon be sold and the money forwarded to him. He had also lent 500 francs to Charles Morice and trusted that he would presently be repaid.

During his first four months in Mataiea he produced about 20 canvases, scenes of everyday native life greatly simplified in form and heightened by brilliant color. Unlike Van Gogh, who delighted in primary colors and in placing complementaries side by side, Gauguin worked in nonprimary hues and juxtaposed those that were closely allied—pink and orange, violet and purple, as in *Man with Axe (page 130)*, achieving strange and beautiful harmonies that few artists had previously dared to attempt.

The Tahitians liked Gauguin and called him "Koké," which was as close as they could come to the pronunciation of his last name. After a suitable time he was introduced to a young girl named Teha'amana, who, with the approval of her mother, became his wife in a simple Tahitian ceremony. The girl was 13, which was considered a marriageable age among the natives. Gauguin was captivated: "I loved her," he wrote, "and told her so, and it brought smiles to her face." Apparently he did indeed love her, as it was not easy to extract such a confession from him. (On a later occasion he said of himself, "To make me say 'I love you'

you will first have to break all my teeth in.") After Teha'amana moved into his hut it became "an abode of happiness. In the morning when the sun rose the house was filled with radiance. Teha'amana's face shone like gold, tingeing everything with its luster, and the two of us would go out and refresh ourselves in the nearby stream as simply and naturally as in the garden of Eden. . . . I no longer saw any difference between good and evil. All was beautiful, and all wonderful." The local gendarme did not agree. He felt that Europeans should not be seen bathing in the nude and warned Gauguin about it.

Teha'amana understood his painting no more than had Mette, but performed all the household tasks with gaiety and was helpful in securing food. She did develop the habit of meeting lovers when she went out into the bush to gather fruit, but even after Gauguin discovered this he was not greatly upset. Teha'amana also served him often as a model. It is she who holds the Christ Child in *I Hail Thee, Mary (page 116)*, and she who appears in *The Spirit of the Dead Watching (pages 132-133)*. This latter painting was actually inspired by Teha'amana, for she introduced him to a few of the superstitions of the Tahitians, including the fear of *tupapaus*, or ghosts, that attempt to invade unlighted houses at night. Gauguin's description of the idea behind the work should have been particularly pleasing to his Symbolist friends in France. He related that he had been absent from his hut after sundown and had returned to find the girl lying terrified on her bed in the dark. Lacking means to strike a light, she was convinced that the waiting *tupapau* was about to enter at any moment.

"How does a native woman envisage a specter?" he wrote. "She has never visited a theater or read novels. When she tries to imagine one, therefore, she has to think of some [ordinary] person she has seen. So my specter is just like an ordinary little woman stretching out her hand as if to seize the prey. My feeling for the decorative leads me to strew the background with flowers. These are *tupapau* flowers (phosphorescent lights). . . . Let me sum up. The musical composition: undulating lines, harmonies of orange and blue connected by the secondary colors of yellow and violet, and lit by greenish sparks. The literary theme: the soul of the living woman united with the spirit of the dead. The opposites of night and day. I have set down the origin of this picture for those who must always know the why and wherefore. But otherwise it is simply a nude from the South Seas."

Despite his enchantment with Teha'amana, Gauguin remained a lonely man in Tahiti. Self-exiled from the white community, he was also a foreigner among the natives. He wrote affectionately to Mette and filled a notebook with aphorisms suggesting ideas that he thought were shared by his daughter Aline, inscribing it, "These ruminations are reflections of myself. She, too, is a savage; she will understand me."

Although life in Mataiea was somewhat easier than it had been in France, Gauguin still felt the need for money. Occasionally he received a small sum from France but the mail was maddeningly slow—an exchange of letters required four months—and often the news was bleak. His friend Morice not only did not repay the loan of 500 francs but em-

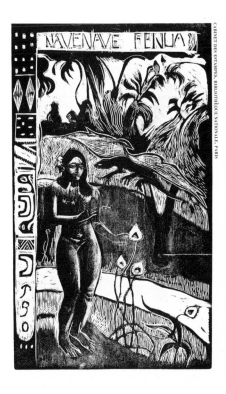

Gauguin conveyed the mystery of a South Seas rain forest in the woodcut above. The Tahitian title means "wonderful earth." The wooden bas-relief below is built around the injunction "Be in love and you will be happy," but the cringing, woeful figures around the words belie the simplicity of that message. The fox, which appears in many of Gauguin's works, was explained by the artist as a symbol of perverseness—and of himself.

bezzled another 850 that had been entrusted to him by an art dealer for forwarding. With some justice, Gauguin felt cut off and betrayed. Moreover, his health began to fail: at 44 he wrote that "I have suddenly aged quite astonishingly." In addition to his syphilis, or perhaps in connection with it, he had developed a heart ailment, and at times was having difficulty with his eyes. Nevertheless, when his supply of canvas was exhausted, he resolutely set about making sculptures in wood.

He managed to sell two of his carvings for 300 francs each but his attempt to support himself by his art in Tahiti was foredoomed. Earlier, he had petitioned the director of the Academy of Arts in Paris requesting repatriation as a "destitute and distressed" French citizen, and after months of paper work he was assigned passage home. He left Teha'amana weeping on the beach. In September 1893, after an absence of 29 months, he was back in Paris. He had produced more than 60 paintings in Tahiti. In view of the success of the sale that had been held before his departure, Gauguin might well have hoped for recognition and money.

The Symbolists again came to his aid and promoted another exhibition of his work, but this time it bordered on disaster. There were only a few sales and the critical notices were devastating. "If you want to entertain your children," said a note in the press, "send them to the Gauguin exhibition. The attractions include colored images of apelike female quadrumanes stretched out on green billiard tables."

Gauguin, who at times was heroically tenacious and at others easily discouraged, confessed to a friend, "I have nothing to hope for here. I should like never to see Europeans again." However, as if to counterbalance his fiasco, he had recently come into a windfall. An uncle who had lived in Orléans, Isidore Gauguin, died and left him 13,000 francs. Mette, who got word of the legacy even before Gauguin did, sent him a telegram and asked for half the money.

While the estate was being settled, Gauguin, who could now borrow money easily, moved into an apartment in Paris. There he held soirees during which he exploited his role as world traveler, discoursing on the South Seas to his guests. These were mainly young artists and writers, but among them were a few men of stature, including Degas, the poet Mallarmé and the young sculptor Aristide Maillol. Occasionally there were music and dancing, and plates of little cakes were passed by Gauguin's new mistress, a dark-skinned half-caste girl, part Malay and part Indian, named Annah. She was indolent, garrulous and childish—although that was only to be expected in view of her age, which was 13. (Gauguin had a predilection for young girls, a desire easy to satisfy in the dissolute Paris of that time, although he also had affairs with mature women.) To keep Annah amused he bought her a pet monkey. He also resumed painting, drawing on his recollections of Tahiti to produce canvases as excellent as those he had made on the island. He worked, as he often said, better from memory than from nature.

After he had been in Paris for several months Gauguin at last received his legacy, but sent Mette only 1,500 francs. The letters that passed between them became increasingly bitter—Mette had friends in

Gauguin shared Toulouse-Lautrec's penchant for whimsical photographs, as this snapshot testifies. It was taken in 1893, after Gauguin had returned from his first trip to Tahiti and was living at the Paris studio of Alphonse Mucha, a Czech artist. Musically inclined, Gauguin owned a French horn, a guitar, and two mandolins. Here he sits at Mucha's harmonium, trouserless but self-possessed.

the city and doubtless had been informed about Annah. The possibility of a reconciliation dwindled to the vanishing point.

In April 1894, shortly before his 46th birthday, Gauguin journeyed again to Brittany in hopes of finding a quiet atmosphere for work but soon met with disaster. While strolling in a seaside town with Annah and a few fellow artists and their ladies, he heard insults being shouted at his half-caste companion from a café. Gauguin reacted, and there was a brawl in which he was knocked down and brutally kicked by several Breton fishermen wearing heavy sabots. His leg was smashed just above the ankle, the shinbone protruding from the skin.

Gauguin was bedridden in Brittany for two months: his injury did not heal properly. When at last he returned to the city, hobbling on a heavy, carved cane, he found that Annah, who had arrived earlier, had ransacked his apartment. She removed everything she considered valuable, but she did not trouble to take his paintings.

"This filthy Europe!" he cried. He would go back to the South Seas and "carve imaginary beings on the trees," ending his life "free and tranquil without thought for the morrow and without struggling eternally against the fools." Before his departure he held another sale, an auction that was even more disastrous than the preceding offering. He was forced to buy back much of his own work because the bidders refused to meet the minimum prices he had set. One of his friends took him to dinner after the debacle and recorded that Gauguin was "crying like a child."

He returned to Tahiti in September 1895 and found that Papeete had become increasingly Europeanized. There were electric lights and a fun fair with a steam-driven merry-go-round. The local newspaper had begun to advance the cause of art—"We have pleasure in offering our readers *four* superb oleographs of J. F. Millet's famous paintings, *The Angelus, The Gleaners, The Sower* and *The Shepherdess and Flock*, which depict rural life in masterly style against a background full of sound and healthy poetry." The taste of middle-class Europe, with its joy in the realistic, the sentimental and the pleasantly narrative, had followed him around the globe.

Gauguin leased a plot of land near Papeete and built a hut. He bought a horse and trap; the wound in his leg had opened and he had difficulty in walking. He summoned Teha'amana, who during his absence had married a Tahitian youth, and she promptly came to him. However, the second honeymoon was brief; the girl was shocked by his physical decay and soon returned to her husband. Gauguin found another vahine, Pau'ura a Tai, whom he described as being 13.

Within a few months Gauguin was again reduced to circumstances identical to those of his first sojourn in Tahiti; his capital exhausted, he waited anxiously for the arrival of every mail schooner, hoping that friends or dealers in Paris had somehow managed to sell a painting. After he had been in the island for a year and a half he heard from Mette, who informed him in briefest terms that his daughter Aline was dead of pneumonia at 19. Gauguin did not reply immediately, but then sent a curt note that concluded, "Her tomb over there with flowers—it

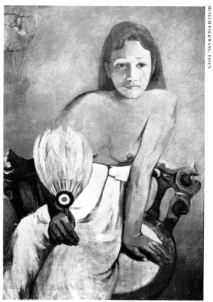

MUSEUM FOLKWANG, ESSEN

The red-haired Tohotaua was one of Gauguin's last models and also his mistress, though she had a native husband. A commercial traveler visiting Gauguin's home, which he called "house of pleasure," photographed her *(top)* while she sat for the painting shown above. Gauguin also produced a portrait of her husband, who posed congenially despite a fearsome local reputation for practicing black magic.

is only an illusion. Her tomb is here near me. My tears are living flowers." He never wrote to his wife again.

Late in 1897, about eight months after hearing of Aline's death, Gauguin produced his largest and surely one of his finest paintings— *Where do we come from? What are we? Where are we going? (pages 134-135).* Lacking canvas for so enormous a work—it is nearly five feet high by 13 feet wide—he painted it on the common burlap used in Tahiti for making copra sacks. He evidently intended the painting as a last testament. Shortly after completing it he walked up into the hills behind his hut, taking with him a box of powdered arsenic that had been prescribed as medication for rashes that resulted from his syphilis. He swallowed all of it and lay down to die. But the amount of poison was too great; instead of killing him it acted merely as a painful purgative, and after a night of vomiting and retching he returned to his hut "condemned," as he said, "to live."

During the next two years Gauguin painted little. His health grew worse and the possibility of help from France seemed more remote—although, unknown to him, a market for his paintings was fast developing. He took a job as a clerk in the Tahitian Public Works Department and for a time dabbled in journalism, contributing articles to a satirical monthly called *Les Guêpes (The Wasps)* in which he assailed the colonial government. His complaints were peevish and sometimes obscure —he once charged that a native had been committing a nuisance near his house by "going about in the night with an ordinary house broom and sweeping among the bushes in the grounds," and he was furious at the local magistrate for doing nothing about it. Leaving *Les Guêpes,* he founded his own paper, *Le Sourire (The Smile),* which consisted of four pages and had a circulation of 21. In it he continued to attack the administration, referring to various public figures as bogeymen and despots.

In May 1900, aged 51, Gauguin was rescued from his painful poverty by a Parisian art dealer named Ambroise Vollard, who agreed to buy all of Gauguin's future paintings at 200 francs apiece and to advance him 300 francs a month against production. Secure at last, Gauguin sold his hut in Tahiti and embarked for the island of Hiva Oa in the Marquesas, about 750 miles to the northeast, where he hoped to find a more unspoiled society and better models, as he said.

The Marquesas Islands, although they lacked an amusement park, still had a claim to civilization. Their population, which had been about 80,000 when American and European vessels had begun to frequent them early in the 19th Century, had dwindled to 3,500 by the time Gauguin arrived, owing to such involuntary imports as tuberculosis, alcoholism and measles, which was very often fatal to the previously unexposed natives. Gauguin, with the aid of native carpenters, built a house on Hiva Oa, decorating its interior with a collection of pornographic photographs he had bought in Suez. He soon acquired a new mistress, aged 14, and he began to paint once more.

Unfortunately he continued his quarrel with the colonial administrators—in Hiva Oa there was a gendarme who was responsible to the authorities in Tahiti. Gauguin frequently offended the man, who once issued him a summons for driving a cart at night without lights. Since Gauguin's cart was the only one on the island, it could not have been a great menace to traffic, and thus it is possible to believe that he somehow went out of his way to insult the policeman.

His various diseases became worse, and he wrote to France suggesting that he return home. In reply he received a letter from a friend: "It is to be feared that your arrival would upset a tendency, an incubation, which is taking place in public opinion with regard to you: you are at the moment that extraordinary, legendary artist who, from the far Pacific, sends disconcerting, inimitable works . . . you have passed into *the history of art. . . .* Wait patiently."

Gauguin evidently shrugged and continued his quarrels with the local authorities—or rather with the world itself. Bitter, quietly desperate, he assailed a Catholic priest who had attempted to prevent young girls from visiting his hut. With more justice Gauguin also attacked the Church for having snatched most of the good land on Hiva Oa, sometimes obtaining it by promising the natives better real estate in the next world. His belligerence led to serious problems. On a trumped-up charge, which more reflected wrath than reality, he was convicted of libeling the local gendarme and sentenced to three months in jail.

The sentence was never served. Gauguin appealed. "I shall always hold my head high," he said, "proud of my well-earned reputation. Nor shall I permit anyone to say anything derogatory to my honor." Before the appeal was heard Paul Gauguin died, alone in his hut. It is recorded that a native found him and "bit him in the head," which was thought in the Marquesas to be a means of rousing the moribund, as well it might have been.

The Catholic priest, reporting to France, wrote that "the only noteworthy event here has been the sudden death of a contemptible individual named Gauguin, a reputed artist but an enemy of God and everything that is decent."

At about the same time a French functionary in the Marquesas wrote, "I have requested all creditors of the deceased to submit duplicate statements of their accounts, but am already convinced that the liabilities will considerably exceed the assets, as the few pictures left by the late painter, who belonged to the decadent school, have little prospect of finding purchasers." Gauguin had sent most of his paintings to France but a few still remained in Hiva Oa. These, together with many drawings, watercolors and wood carvings that were found in his house, were auctioned in Tahiti for the benefit of his creditors. Prices were low. One canvas, *Breton Village in the Snow,* sold for seven francs. The auctioneer held it upside down and announced that it was a picture of Niagara Falls.

Gauguin was buried in a hilltop cemetery in Hiva Oa overlooking the water, having lived not quite 55 years. A young Marquesan friend placed a baked-clay memorial on his grave: PAUL GAUGUIN, 1903. This remained for more than half a century but was stolen a few years ago, perhaps by a tourist who wished to take home a souvenir of the South Seas.

Standing beside one of his father's paintings in a New York museum is Émile Gauguin —one of Paul's illegitimate children, who became an artist in his own right. His Polynesian mother, Pau'ura a Tai, was 17 when he was born in 1899. Gauguin was 51. Émile grew up to be a fisherman. Then, in 1961, he was discovered by a French woman journalist and encouraged by her to try painting. His wildly colorful canvases caused some interest in the art world, and Émile was brought to the United States, where he sold some of his works. But after several years he missed his large family and decided to return to his island home.

Troubled Idyl

In the spring of 1891 Gauguin sailed for Tahiti. He had evidently convinced himself, as he had before, that in a new environment where the living was simple and cheap he would find a perfect place to work. During the previous months, beset by financial worries and exhausted by his burst of activity in Brittany, he had scarcely painted at all. Now, he imagined, he could live off the natural bounty of the island, where his flagging inspiration would be refreshed by a wild and primitive beauty, and where his family and a host of artist-friends would soon join him.

But the reality of Tahiti was far different from Gauguin's dream. Arriving in Papeete, the capital city, he found it far too civilized and moved into the back country. There, indeed, he was inspired by the sturdy Polynesian men and women and he found himself fascinated by their ancient myths and superstitions. He completed some 65 canvases in about 18 months. The living, however, was not so easy as he had anticipated. Unable to gather his own food, as the natives did, he was forced to buy at relatively high prices from the few local stores. Money owed him in France was not forthcoming. Worse, his health was not good and his eyes began to fail. So, in 1893, he returned to Europe. But Paris, and even his beloved Brittany, did not welcome him and in 1895 he fled again to the South Seas. At least in the islands he could paint, and it was in his work—his glorious, richly colored pictures—that he found his final escape.

Never moved to paint the tight-laced, frivolous Parisiennes of his time, Gauguin was entranced until his dying day by the animal grace and carefree nudity of Polynesian women, and he celebrated their womanhood in a flood of pictures like the one at right.

Paul Gauguin: *Tahitian Women with Mango Blossoms,* 1899

Paul Gauguin: *Man with Axe*, 1891

Paul Gauguin: *Fatata te Miti (By the Sea)*, 1892

Soon after his arrival in the tropics, Gauguin's style began to change subtly. The picture at the left is one of the first he painted in Tahiti, and it still shows the stained-glass kind of outlining of figures and forms that had characterized some of his Breton works *(pages 81, 86)*. Within a year, however, he had relaxed this formal device somewhat, and in the painting above, the colors meet each other in easy curves and graceful abstract shapes. In both pictures Gauguin continued to pursue his "synthetic" use of color—colors used for their own sake or as symbolic of an emotion or thought. At the left, for instance, the sandy beach is seen in stripes of green, red and purple, the nets the woman is arranging in the canoe are a golden heap. The choices seem arbitrary, but they are highly personal and always harmonize. A hint

at how Gauguin arrived at his colors is found in his journal, *Noa Noa*. He described the scene that had inspired this picture, writing of the heavy axe "which leaves a blue impression against the silvery sky."

While he lived in Tahiti, Gauguin used color more and more for its own glorious sake, abstractly and musically like a composer. Indeed, as one of his poet friends said of a picture, perhaps the one above, "It is a musical poem, it needs no libretto." Gauguin's paintings always have a "libretto"; they are not pure abstractions. The subject matter of the two shown here is perfectly clear. But Gauguin was also interested in the spiritual life of the "savages" that he came to know and love. In other works he would delve deeply into their lore, their beliefs, and into his own feelings about the mysteries of life.

Gauguin took a wife in Tahiti, a 13-year-old girl called Teha'amana, and it was partly from her that he learned how some of the old myths and superstitions lingered beneath the mask of Christianity that the islanders had only recently adopted. Among the powers and spirits that were very real to the Tahitians were *tupapaus*, ghosts that stalked the night and represented the Spirit of the Dead. Gauguin witnessed the potency of this belief one night when he returned late to his hut to find his child bride in the dark stretched out on her bed half-crazed with fear. Tahitian women, it seems, never slept without a light during the night and Gauguin had run out of lamp oil—one reason for his being away. The image of the poor girl so struck the painter that he set about to re-create the scene on canvas.

In essence, the painting is a repetition of a classic subject—the reclining nude. Gauguin had once copied Manet's *Olympia*, and he certainly knew the elegant and lovely Venuses of Titian and Velázquez, perhaps even Goya's *Naked Maja*. But in most other respects the picture is pure Gauguin. The decorative patterns of the bed cloth, the flat, background wall studded with phosphorescent flowers—symbolic of the eerie glow of the spirit—these are elements of his style as it had developed in Brittany. Similarly personal is his invention of a physical form for the *tupapau*, shown as a mask-faced woman seated at the foot of the bed. Uniting symbol and reality, he has painted a picture full of beauty and meaning.

132

Paul Gauguin: *Manao Tupapau (The Spirit of the Dead Watching)*, 1892

133

In 1897, two years after returning to the South Seas from an unhappy sojourn in France, Gauguin was again plagued by poverty and disease and decided on the ultimate escape: suicide. But first he wished to sum up his ideas in one last, great painting. It is his largest— more than 12 feet wide—and perhaps his finest work.

Here is his own description of the picture, which reads from right to left, in the Oriental fashion. "To the right, below, a sleeping baby and three seated women. Two figures dressed in purple confide their thoughts to each other. An enormous [seated] figure which intentionally violates perspective, raises its arm in the air and looks in

astonishment at these two people who dare to think of their destiny. A figure in the center is picking fruit. Two cats near a child. A . . . goat. An idol, both arms mysteriously and rhythmically raised, seems to indicate the Beyond. A . . . girl seems to listen to the idol. Lastly, an old woman approaching death appears . . . resigned to her thoughts. She completes the story. At her feet a strange white bird . . . represents the futility of words."

The title of the picture, seen by Gauguin as a philosophical statement "comparable to the Gospels," reveals his pessimistic mood. But Gauguin's suicide attempt failed; he lived—and painted—five more years.

Paul Gauguin: *Where do we come from? What are we? Where are we going?* 1897

VII

Mastery
out of Despair

When Vincent regained consciousness in the hospital in Arles it was not the fact that he had suffered a severe mental breakdown that first concerned him. Nor was he greatly troubled by his mutilated ear—soon he was able to joke about having one made of papier-mâché. His deep fear was that Gauguin might send a telegram to Theo, alarming him over what Vincent considered a trivial affair. Gauguin did. He refused to see Vincent and telegraphed Theo, who took the first train to Arles, arriving late on Christmas Eve. Theo remained with Vincent for two or three days but then—accompanied by Gauguin—returned sadly to Paris. He had seen enough to know that there was nothing he could do for his brother.

Theo had just become engaged to a Dutch girl, Johanna Bonger from Amsterdam, and in a letter to her he now reported how matters stood with Vincent. "He had, while I was with him, moments in which he acted normally, but then after a short while he slipped off into wanderings on philosophy and theology. It was deeply saddening to witness all this, for from time to time he became conscious of his illness and in those moments he tried to cry—yet no tears came. Poor fighter and poor, poor sufferer. For the time being nobody can do anything to alleviate his suffering, though he himself feels it deeply and strongly. If he had been able to find somebody to whom he could have opened his heart, maybe it would never have come to all this."

Next day Theo added, "There is little hope, but during his life he has done more than many others, and he has suffered and struggled more than most people could have done. If it must be that he dies, so be it, but my heart breaks when I think of it."

Vincent's tragedy aroused the sympathy of some of the townspeople. His friend, the postman Joseph Roulin, visited him daily and remained in frequent touch with Theo. So too did his physician, Dr. Felix Rey, and the local Protestant minister, Pastor Frederic Salles. On December 29th Dr. Rey wrote to Theo that Vincent's condition was grave—he had tried to bathe in a coal scuttle, had menaced a nurse, and had lain down in another patient's bed and refused to get up. It had been nec-

It was Van Gogh's habit whenever he arrived at a new place to record the scenes he saw about him every day. Thus, when he began his voluntary confinement in the mental hospital at Saint-Rémy, he sketched and painted many views of the grounds, including this delicate watercolor.

Stone Steps in the Hospital Garden, Saint-Rémy, May 1889

137

essary to lock him up. But only three days later Vincent was so recovered that he could write to Theo: "I expect to start work again soon. The char-woman and my friend Roulin have taken care of the house, and have put everything in order. When I get out, I shall be able to go my own lit-tle way here again, and soon the fine weather will be coming and I shall again start on the orchards in bloom. My dear boy, I am so terribly dis-tressed over your journey. I should have wished you had been spared that, for after all no harm came to me, and there was no reason why you should be so upset."

To this letter Vincent added a postscript for Gauguin: "Look here—was my brother Theo's journey really necessary, old man? Now at least do reassure him completely, and I entreat you, be confident yourself that after all no evil exists in this best of worlds in which everything is for the best."

In this last sentence Vincent revealed his childlike vulnerability by paraphrasing the famous saying of the fatuously optimistic philosopher, Dr. Pangloss, in Voltaire's satire, *Candide.* In the face of repeated and horrendous catastrophes, Pangloss keeps insisting that "all is for the best in this best of all possible worlds." Voltaire's point, to be sure, is that Pangloss is a fool and that this is the worst of all possible worlds. But Vincent, with his naïve—or heroic—idealism, chose to take Dr. Pan-gloss seriously. In his letters he referred to Pangloss' philosophy many times, and it is plain that he often agreed with it. Despite his own mis-fortunes, Vincent wanted to believe that everything *is* for the best in this best of all possible worlds.

From the letters written immediately after his seizure it seems clear that Vincent had as yet almost no idea of what had happened to him. He soon wrote to Theo, "I hope I have just had simply an artist's fit, and then a lot of fever after *very* considerable loss of blood, as an ar-tery was severed; but my appetite came back at once, my digestion is all right and my blood recovers from day to day, and in the same way se-renity returns. . . . So please quite deliberately forget your unhappy jour-ney and my illness." A few weeks later he revealed, "I knew well enough that one could fracture one's legs and arms and recover af-terward, but I did not know that you could fracture the brain in your head and recover from that too." By this time it seemed that he had, in-deed, recovered: he had resumed living in his yellow house and was painting again. Moreover, his art showed not the slightest trace of mad-ness. His *Self-Portrait with Pipe and Bandaged Ear (page 169)* is a mas-terpiece of objectivity and his likenesses of Madame Roulin, the postman's wife *(La Berceuse),* made at about this time, are as lucid and brilliantly constructed as any of his works.

Early in February 1889, a month after his release from the hospital, Vincent suffered a relapse. As had happened in his first attack, he found himself terrified by unearthly sounds and voices, and now was convinced that someone was attempting to poison him. When he was readmitted to the hospital he refused to speak a word. But again he recovered and soon returned to work. He still resisted the thought that his condition might be chronic, and eagerly snatched at a suggestion that acts of madness were not rare in the Midi. In a letter to Theo he reported that he had found encouragement for this optimistic idea in, of all places, the nightmarish brothel that he had visited on the night of his self-mutilation: "Yesterday I went to see the girl I had gone to when I was out of my wits. They told me there that in this country things like that are not out of the ordinary."

Many of the proper people of Arles, however, were not so compassionate as the girls in the bordello. Swarms of children, sometimes accompanied by adults, jeered him in the streets. When he retreated into his yellow house they threw stones at it and climbed up to taunt him through the windows. Goaded beyond endurance, he screamed at them. Soon the police came to the house, seized him and took him once more to the hospital, where he was locked in a cell for dangerous lunatics. More than 80 citizens—none of them, he later discovered, his immediate neighbors—had signed a letter to the mayor requesting that action. "What a staggering blow between the eyes it was," he wrote, "to find so many people here cowardly enough to join together against one man, and that man ill."

In his cell, peered at by guards, deprived of his paints and even of his tobacco, he was able to assure Theo that he was "in full possession of my faculties, not a madman but the brother you know." He was also able to add a few words of comfort: "the best we can do perhaps is to make fun of our petty griefs and, in a way, of the great griefs of human life too. Take it like a man, go straight to your goal. . . . Goodbye, my dear boy, for a little while, I hope, and don't worry. Perhaps it is a sort of quarantine they are forcing on me, for all I know." Not long afterward Vincent wrote to his sister Wilhelmina in Holland: "You don't know the arguments of the good Father Pangloss in Voltaire's *Candide*. . . . But the memory of them often sustains me in the hours and days and nights that are hardly easy or enviable."

Theo, preparing for his marriage, could ill afford a second journey to Arles, but on learning that the artist Paul Signac was about to travel to southern France asked him to visit Vincent. Signac was allowed by the hospital authorities to escort him on a walk. They went to the yellow house, found it sealed and guarded by police, but eventually gained admission. Vincent happily displayed his pictures, and as Signac recalled, "All day long he talked about painting, literature, socialism. In the evening he was a little tired. There was a terrific mistral blowing which may have unnerved him. He wanted to drink a liter of turpentine directly out of the container which was on the table of the bedroom. It was time for him to return to the hospital."

Vincent continued to hope that his seizures had a simple origin, and that rest and a cautious life might cure him. "M. Rey says that instead of eating enough and at regular times, I kept myself going on coffee and alcohol. I admit all that, but all the same it is true that to attain the high yellow note I attained last summer, I really had to be pretty well keyed up." And that much is certainly correct: to produce his pictures in "the furnace heat . . . of the Midi," venturing into the perilous world where objects and emotions become fused, he had gambled his san-

The hospital at Arles looks today much as it did when Van Gogh was twice confined there in 1889. A sun-whitened Mediterranean stucco building, its shaded galleries open onto a landscaped courtyard and round pool, which Van Gogh painted while he was recuperating from his seizure. Vincent's room was on the second floor of the three-story building.

A recent photograph of the Catholic asylum of Saint-Rémy, where Van Gogh was a patient, shows the imposing façade of the rambling old structure. The asylum was originally an Augustinian monastery built in the 12th and 13th Centuries. Two long, low wings extending from each side of the cloister served to house patients when the asylum was founded early in the 1800s. Vincent's drawing of the circular stone pool is on page 157.

ity. Each day he had left the fields with his canvas and easel, reeling from "the mental labor of balancing the six essential colors—red, blue, yellow, orange, lilac, green. Sheer work and calculation . . . like an actor on a stage in a difficult part, with a hundred things to think of at once in a single half-hour."

After Signac's visit Vincent was once more permitted to walk abroad by himself and to paint. His physical strength increased, but he found himself filled with "a certain undercurrent of vague sadness difficult to define," troubled by shapeless fears—"My God, those anxieties—who can live in the modern world without catching his share of them?" He continued to live in the hospital and could not face the terrors of striking out again on his own. The Protestant minister, the Reverend Frederic Salles, told him of a mental institution in the town of Saint-Rémy, about 15 miles away, where he might be accepted as a patient. Voluntarily, indeed eagerly, Vincent requested admission to the place, hoping only that he would be allowed to continue painting. At first it appeared that the director of Saint-Rémy, Dr. Théophile Peyron, might not permit this. In despair Vincent spoke seriously of enlisting for five years in the French Foreign Legion—possibly he might be able to do a little painting there, and military routine would organize the horrors of daily life even more neatly than the order of an institution for the mad. It was the unscheduled horror, the panic that suddenly seizes a lonely man unprotected by any uniform, with which he could not cope. But at length an arrangement was made with the hospital at Saint-Rémy. Theo wrote to the director: "With the consent of the person in question, who is my brother, I request the admission to your institution of Vincent Willem van Gogh, painter, 36 years old. . . . In view of the fact that his internment is desired mainly to prevent the recurrence of previous attacks and not because his mental condition is unsound, I hope

that you will find it possible to permit him to do some painting outside of your establishment. . . . I beg you to be kind enough to allow him at least a half liter of wine with his meals."

Vincent was admitted to the Saint-Rémy hospital on May 8, 1889. Director Peyron interviewed him at that time, and entered in the register that the patient "is suffering from acute mania with hallucinations of sight and hearing which have caused him to mutilate himself by cutting off his ear. At present he seems to have recovered his reason, but he does not feel that he possesses the strength and the courage to live independently . . . my opinion is that M. van Gogh is subject to epileptic fits at very infrequent intervals."

An exact diagnosis of Vincent's ailment can never be set forth—no accurate case history was recorded by any of the doctors in whose care he found himself. In the years since his death, however, many physicians, psychoanalysts and psychologists have been bold enough to offer their speculations. It has been suggested that he suffered from paranoid schizophrenia, that he was an advanced alcoholic and that his brain was damaged by syphilis, but there does not appear to be much foundation for any of these notions. It has been generally thought that Dr. Peyron of Saint-Rémy, in his use of the word "epileptic," may have been fairly close to the mark. The physician who had attended Vincent in Arles after his first attack was also persuaded that epilepsy was involved. However, the word can have a variety of connotations, and it would be presumptuous to fasten on any one of them. In recent years psychiatrists have also favored the view that Vincent had a "manic-depressive psychosis"—he did, it is true, experience alternating periods of depression and intense activity. But for that matter the lives of most people have a similar pattern, with the obvious exception that the average citizen never reaches such depths or heights. Perhaps the most rea-

A view of the rear of Saint-Rémy, where a vineyard has been planted, shows the tower that was part of the original monastery. Vincent's cell-like room was on the second floor of the wing at the right. The wing has been unused for decades and is due to be rebuilt. There is a memorial to the artist on the hospital grounds, but no attempt has been made to preserve the room Vincent used.

Grim corridors in the wing at Saint-Rémy where Van Gogh lived give access to rows of bolted cells *(above)* with barred windows. Aside from confinement, which was probably prescribed for his own safety, Vincent received no other treatment than therapeutic baths in a stone tub. However, he was given a certain amount of freedom to roam the hospital grounds for exercise and to paint and sketch.

sonable view is that of the Dutch psychiatrist Dr. G. Kraus, whose opinion is appended to the American edition of Vincent's letters. Dr. Kraus, after considering and rejecting a number of hypotheses, refuses to give Van Gogh's ailment any name at all, concluding simply that "he was an individual in his illness, as well as in his art."

Vincent's attacks were totally overpowering, and seem to have been triggered by severe emotional stress—as after his disastrous contact with Gauguin or at times when he feared he might lose Theo's support. During the worst parts of his seizures he was incapable of drawing, painting or writing, but when he recovered he was as lucid as ever. Thus it is vain to look for signs of madness in his art or letters; there are none. There were changes in his art at Saint-Rémy, but these were anticipated in the pictorial problems he had set for himself long before his attack and probably would have occurred whether he had been ill or not. Other changes can be attributed not to insanity but to his natural anxieties. It is scarcely surprising that he should have been profoundly worried, or that his choice of subjects and his technique should at times have reflected this.

At Saint-Rémy he received almost no treatment for his illness. Even if the director of medicine in the hospital, Dr. Peyron, had been a particularly enlightened man, which he was not, the necessary knowledge was not available in 1889. Hydrotherapy was the standard procedure. Twice a week, in two-hour sessions, Vincent was soaked in a tub of water; his letters mention no other attempts at cure.

The hospital at Saint-Rémy, which is still in use, is operated by Catholic nuns. Once a monastery, it incorporates a cloister and chapel dating as far back as the 13th Century. The walled grounds include two long and grimly institutional dormitories for men and women. There are bars on the windows; the corridors are dim and appear endless. A park-like enclosure in front of the hospital, weedy and unkempt, contains a circular fountain and a few stone benches. In the distance can be seen a line of wild, jagged limestone hills called the Alpilles; close at hand are small fields, cultivated in Vincent's time but now largely fallow. The air is extremely clear and very still. When a bell is struck the sound quivers overhead for a long time and the slowly wandering patients seem inclined to glance upward as though looking for a new color in the sky.

Vincent was assigned not one room but two, one for sleeping and another for painting. There were many vacancies in the men's dormitory, which then had only about 10 occupants. In his first letters he described his surroundings and his feelings: "Though there are some very seriously ill patients here, the fear and horror of madness that I used to have has already lessened a great deal. And though you continually hear terrible howls and cries like those of beasts in a menagerie, in spite of that people get to know each other very well and help each other when their attacks come on. When I am working in the garden they all come to look, and I assure you they have the discretion and manners to leave me alone—more than the good people of the town of Arles, for instance. . . .

"I have a little [bedroom] with greenish-gray paper and two curtains of sea-green with a design of very pale roses, brightened by slight touches of blood-red. These curtains, probably the relics of some rich and deceased patient, are very pretty in design. A worn armchair probably comes from the same source. . . . Through the iron-barred window I see a square field of wheat in an enclosure, a perspective as in Van Goyen, above which I see the morning sun rising in all its glory. . . .

"The food is so-so. Naturally it tastes rather moldy, as in a cockroach-infested restaurant in Paris or in a boardinghouse." (Vincent revealed, months later, that he had been unable to choke down the unpalatable hospital fare and had subsisted almost entirely on bread and soup; only in the aftermaths of his attacks was he supplied with extra rations of meat and wine.)

"The room where we stay on wet days is like a third-class waiting room in some stagnant village, the more so as there are some distinguished lunatics who always have a hat, spectacles, cane and traveling cloak, almost like at a watering place, and they represent the passengers.

"I am again—speaking of my condition—so grateful for another thing. I gather from others that during their attacks they have also heard strange sounds and voices as I did, and that in their eyes too things seemed to be changing. And that lessens the horror that I retained at first of the attack I have had, and which, when it comes on you unawares, cannot but frighten you beyond measure. Once you know that it is part of the disease, you take it like anything else. If I had not seen other lunatics close up, I should not have been able to free myself from dwelling on it constantly."

Within a few weeks after his admission to the hospital Vincent—accompanied by a guard—was allowed to go out into the countryside to paint. He became fascinated with the Provençal cypress trees, which "are always occupying my thoughts, I should like to make something of them like the canvases of the sunflowers, because it astonishes me that they have not yet been done as I see them. The tree is as beautiful of line and proportion as an Egyptian obelisk. And the green has a quality of such distinction. It is a splash of *black* in a sunny landscape, but it is one of the most interesting black notes, and the most difficult to hit off exactly that I can imagine."

Although "obelisk" suggests straight-sided symmetry, Vincent in fact saw the cypresses as writhing black flames spurting up out of the troubled earth. His treatment of them is so personal and so strong that cypresses today seem almost his private property. It would be a very brave, perhaps foolhardy artist who would try to surpass the painting on page 170. No doubt Vincent was attracted to cypresses because their wind-tormented shapes echoed his own mood. At Saint-Rémy he was powerfully drawn to nature under stress: huge whirling clouds, bent and gesticulating trees, hills and ravines alive and turbulent. Sometimes he combined this agitation with quiet sadness, as in his painting of the garden at the asylum: "Now the nearest tree is an enormous trunk, struck by lightning and sawed off. But one side branch shoots up very high and lets fall an avalanche of dark green pine needles. This somber giant—like a defeated proud man—contrasts, when considered in the nature of a living creature, with the pale smile of a last rose on the fading bush in front of him. Underneath the trees, empty stone benches, sullen box trees; the sky is mirrored—yellow—in a puddle left by the rain. A sunbeam, the last ray of daylight, raises the somber ocher almost to orange. Here and there small figures wander around among the tree trunks.

"You will realize that this combination of red-ocher, of green gloomed over by gray, the black streaks surrounding the contours, produces something of the sensation of anguish, called *noir-rouge*, from which certain of my companions in misfortune frequently suffer. Moreover the motif of the great tree struck by lightning, the sickly green-pink smile of the last flower of autumn serve to confirm this impression."

By early July 1889, when he had been in the asylum for two months, Vincent felt stable enough to make a day's round trip (again, with a guard) to Arles to fetch some canvases that were still in storage there. Before his departure he had a conversation with Dr. Peyron, a man who evidently did not believe in good cheer and optimism. He told Vincent that he "must wait a year before thinking myself cured, as the least little thing might bring on another attack." However, in recent weeks he had had some small cause for hope—his work was going well, and in the evenings he was happily reading (in English) the history plays of Shakespeare that he had asked Theo to send him. Theo had then been married for four months and his wife had just written to Vincent: "I am now going to tell you a great piece of news, on which we have concentrated a good deal of our attention lately—it is that next winter, toward February probably, we hope to have a baby, a pretty little boy—whom we are going to call Vincent, if you will kindly consent to be his godfather. Of course I know we must not count on it too much, and that it may well be a little girl, but Theo and I cannot help imagining that the baby will be a boy."

Buoyed by such events of the previous days, Vincent made the journey to Arles without mishap, but soon after his return he suffered another fit. It is impossible to say what its immediate cause may have been, but its timing is intriguing to those who have made a business, indeed almost an industry, of probing Van Gogh's psyche. Some of these analysts hold that Vincent was jealous and upset by his brother's marriage, and even more by the news of the unborn child. But there is nothing in his letters to support this. He did in fact say, "I am so glad that if there are sometimes cockroaches in the food here, you have your wife and child at home," a remark that appears at first glance to be altogether vicious, sarcastic and self-pitying. But he did not know the use of sarcasm; he truly meant that he could abide the roaches because, in this best of worlds, his brother had cause for happiness. His idealism cannot be overestimated.

Although Vincent never expressed the slightest jealousy or fear that he would lose his brother's affection because of the marriage or the news of a child, it is likely that he was afraid of something else: he might lose his financial support. At any rate this was the opinion of a man who was in a position to know a good deal of the family history. Theo's child was, as his parents had hoped, a boy, and was given Vincent's name. The "child," Mr. Vincent Willem van Gogh, was still living in Holland in 1969. Mr. van Gogh, a 79-year-old retired engineer, pointed out that "the trouble with Gauguin in Arles started right after Vincent heard from Theo that he intended to marry. Other crises came about after Theo's marriage, after the announcement that a baby was expected and after his birth. It must have passed through his mind that he would lose his support, though he never mentioned it and it never came about." Mr. van Gogh's point is well worth bearing in mind, particularly in regard to the sequence of events and Vincent's state of mind when he committed suicide.

Vincent's first attack in Saint-Rémy after the visit to Arles was a severe one. Had it not been for the presence of guards he might have killed himself—apparently he tried to swallow his poisonous paints. In his letters he could not describe his hallucinations in detail because he could not remember them, but later he managed to set down this: "When you suffer much, you see everybody at a great distance, and as at the far end of a room or an immense arena—the very voices seem to come from afar. During the attacks I experience this to such a degree that all the persons I see then, even if I recognize them, which is not always the case, seem to come toward me out of a great distance, and to be quite different from what they are in reality."

Several weeks passed before he recovered, and even when he was lucid again he was almost immobile. "It is splendid weather outside," he wrote, "but for a long time—two months to be exact—I have not left my room; I don't know why." He resumed painting indoors, copying prints after Delacroix, Millet and Rembrandt that Theo sent him. Work, he felt, was his salvation and protection, "the lightning-rod for

During the time Gauguin and Van Gogh lived together in Arles, they often used the same local people as models. While Van Gogh was working on a painting *(top)* of Madame Ginoux, wife of a local café owner, Gauguin made a quick sketch of her *(center)*. Afterward, when Vincent was confined at Saint-Rémy and had no one to sit for him, he made four more paintings of Madame Ginoux, including the one at bottom, this time using Gauguin's sketch as his model.

my illness." But whenever he wished to paint he was obliged to ask permission from the asylum authorities, a situation he found humiliating. (There is no record that anyone in Saint-Rémy liked his art. The nuns certainly did not, but later they complimented his memory in their fashion by saying that he had been polite and submissive.)

As his strength returned, Van Gogh produced one of the few pictures in all his art that suggests death. During the preceding year he had occasionally grazed the subject of suicide in his letters, but had made no threat of it. "Every day I take the remedy which the incomparable Dickens prescribes against suicide. It consists of a glass of wine, a piece of bread with cheese and a pipe of tobacco. This is not complicated, you will tell me, and you will hardly be able to believe that this is the limit to which melancholy will take me; all the same, at some moments—oh, dear me. . . .

"Well, it is not always pleasant, but I do my best not to forget altogether how to make contemptuous fun of it. I try to avoid anything that has any connection with heroism or martyrdom; in short, I do my best not to take lugubrious things lugubriously."

In this particular painting, one of many studies he made of the walled, cultivated field that was visible from his window, he presented death in a warm light. "I am struggling with a canvas begun some days before my indisposition, a 'Reaper'; the study is all yellow, terribly thickly painted, but the subject is fine and simple. For I see this reaper—a vague figure fighting like the devil in the midst of the heat to get to the end of his task—I see in him the image of death, in the sense that humanity might be the wheat he is reaping. . . . But there's nothing sad in this death, it goes its way in broad daylight with a sun flooding everything with a light of pure gold . . . it is an image of death as the great book of nature speaks of it—but what I have sought is the 'almost smiling' . . . I find it queer that I saw it like this from between the iron bars of a cell."

In spite of the mood of the painting, Vincent's thoughts were by no means fixed continually on death or resignation. On the contrary, his will to survive and to continue his work became stronger. He wrote to Theo: "Life passes like this, time does not return, but I am dead set on my work, for just this very reason, that I know the opportunities of working do not return. Especially in my case, in which a more violent attack may forever destroy my power to paint.

"During the attacks I feel cowardly toward the pain and suffering—more of a coward than I ought to be, and it is perhaps this very moral cowardice which, whereas I had no desire to get better before, makes me eat like two now, work hard, limit my relations with the other patients for fear of a relapse—altogether I am now trying to recover like a man who meant to commit suicide and, finding the water too cold, tries to regain the bank."

Vincent remained in the asylum for a year, producing canvases at an average of two a week despite his recurrent attacks. In time, however, he became convinced that his health was being made worse, not better, by his continuing presence in Saint-Rémy. When he asked the medical

146

director for some encouragement about his illness, he received only a bland, "Well, let us hope for the best." In addition, he found the faith of the Catholic nuns superstitious and stifling—the atmosphere was so heavy with it that he began to have religious hallucinations, which he found particularly terrifying.

Increasingly his thoughts tended toward the north and home. He wrote more frequently to his 70-year-old mother in Holland and re-marked that no matter how far he had wandered he would always remain a peasant filled with "something of the Brabant fields and heath." His rec-ollections of his childhood were so strong that he could say, "During my illness I saw again every room in the house at Zundert, every path, every plant in the garden, the view of the fields outside, the neighbors, the graveyard, the church, our kitchen garden at the back—down to a magpie's nest in a tall acacia in the graveyard."

In the midst of this period of melancholy reverie, on January 31, 1890, Theo's son was born. Vincent, unable to go to Paris to see the child, made an exquisite painting as a gift for him: almond branches flow-ering against a blue sky. But almost before it was finished his illness re-turned: "My work was going well, the last canvas of branches in blossom —you will see that it was perhaps the best, the most patiently worked thing I had done, painted with calm and a greater firmness of touch. And the next day, down like a brute. Difficult to understand, things like that, but alas!"

It seemed crucial to Vincent that he leave Saint-Rémy, but he was still reluctant to risk living alone. He thought briefly of going to visit Paul Gauguin, who was then painting in Brittany. When Vincent broached the subject, Gauguin replied with great restraint: "I must admit that I believe it would be possible, very possible, for us to live to-gether, but only with a great many precautions. Your ailing condition, which is not yet completely cured, calls for calm and a lot of fore-thought." To another of his friends, however, Gauguin said what he real-ly thought: "My God! Not that man! He tried to kill me."

Vincent did not press the matter. He asked Theo whether it might be possible to make an arrangement with Camille Pissarro, the wise and be-nevolent Impressionist painter who had befriended him in Paris. Pissarro seemed willing, but Theo was dubious. "I don't think," said Theo, "that he has a great deal to say at home, where his wife wears the pants." And this was the case—Madame Pissarro feared the effect that Vincent might have on her children. However, Pissarro advanced another idea. In the small town of Auvers, some 20 miles from Paris on the Oise River, there lived a very sympathetic man named Paul Ga-chet. A physician who had some knowledge of mental illness, Dr. Gachet was a friend of modern artists (including Cézanne as well as Pissarro) and indeed something of an artist himself. He had a press on which he printed his own etchings.

Dr. Gachet did not offer to take Vincent into his house, but did agree to find lodgings for him and to supply such medical care as he could. It seemed an ideal situation. Vincent resolved to go to Auvers, and it was there that he would die.

Van Gogh's Drawings: Color in Line

Oil painting did not consume all of Van Gogh's prodigious artistic energy during the last two years of his life. While at Arles and the mental hospital at Saint-Rémy, he drew regularly, sketching scenes from the neighboring countryside. As with all his art, he brought to his drawing a mastery of style and an extraordinary technical facility. As a result, much of his graphic work is every bit as strong as his best oils.

Even when working in monochrome, Van Gogh could endow his drawings with the depth, resolution and feel of color. He did this through a skilled use of sinuous lines, hatched strokes and patterns of dots. One of his landscapes in particular *(pages 152-153)* is an inventory of the ways he achieved his effects. In the foreground the use of short, broad lines makes the hillside vegetation seem close and coarse; the dappling dots of the fields soften the middle ground; the minutely executed background also helps infuse the drawing with the visual richness of a fine painting. But Vincent's drawings were more than displays of technique. *Cornfield with Reaper (pages 158-159)*, a study for the famous painting of the same name, indicates a chilling awareness of the imminence of death, which he saw as a reaper. Inevitably, all his work sprang from his overpowering creative impulses. "What is drawing?" he asked in a letter. "It is working oneself through an invisible iron wall that seems to stand between what one feels and what one can do."

While he was at the asylum at Saint-Rémy, Vincent sketched the cypress trees that abounded there —in the dynamic spirals, curlicues and undulating lines that characterize his later style. He drew, and painted, cypresses often during his stay at Saint-Rémy, finding a turbulent vitality in their graceful shape and mass.

Cypresses, Saint-Rémy, 1889
THE BROOKLYN MUSEUM, NEW YORK

View of Arles, May 1888

Landscape with Railway Carriages, Telegraph Pole and Crane, Arles, June 1888   151

VINCENT VAN GOGH FOUNDATION, AMSTERDAM

The Crau from Montmajour, May 1888

153

Fishing Boats at Saintes-Maries-de-la-Mer, June 1888

KUNSTARCHIV ARNTZ, HAAG, OBERBAYERN

The Rock at Montmajour, July 1888

155

The Stone Bench and Ivy, Saint-Rémy, May 1889

The Fountain in the Garden of the Hospital, Saint-Rémy, May 1889

Cornfield with Reaper, Saint-Rémy, June 1889

VIII

"A terrible
and maddened genius"

Early in 1890, before he left the asylum at Saint-Rémy, Vincent received two pieces of news that might ordinarily have been encouraging to any artist. In an avant-garde magazine, *Mercure de France,* there appeared the first article ever written about him, and soon thereafter he was informed that one of his paintings—in the first and only public sale he ever made—had been purchased at an exhibition in Brussels.

The article, by a brilliant young critic named G. Albert Aurier, was full of praise. Aurier couched it in an extravagant style, but he had carefully studied Vincent's paintings in Theo's apartment and in Père Tanguy's shop and had made some penetrating observations. "What particularizes all these works," said Aurier, "is the excess, excess in strength, excess in nervousness, in violence of expression . . . in his frequently headstrong simplification of forms, in his insolence in depicting the sun face to face . . . he reveals a powerful being, a male, a bold man, often brutal and sometimes ingenuously delicate . . . a kind of drunken giant, better able to move mountains than to handle *bibelots,* an ebullient brain which irresistibly pours its lava into all the ravines of art, a terrible and maddened genius, often sublime, sometimes grotesque, almost always on the edge of the pathological. . . . His color is unbelievably dazzling. He is, as far as I know, the only painter who perceives the coloration of things with such intensity."

Vincent was distressed by the article, although not for the reason that might be imagined. He did not object to "maddened" or "pathological," but felt that Aurier had been too flattering to him. Although he thanked the young critic and offered him a gift of a painting of cypresses, he insisted that his own position in art was "very secondary." Others' work, he said, was of greater importance—Gauguin, for example. And soon he implored Theo, "Please ask M. Aurier not to write any more articles on my painting . . . it pains me more than he knows."

Vincent's solitary sale chanced to be made in Brussels because there was in that city an organization of 20 artists and writers, *Les Vingt,* who made great efforts to procure for their exhibitions the best canvases available. One of the organizers of the 1890 show had seen

In the spring of 1890, at about the time Theo and his family visited Vincent in Auvers, Theo's wife, Johanna, was photographed with Vincent Willem, her four-month-old son. As an adult, Vincent Willem van Gogh *(below)* followed neither the career of his father nor that of his uncle, becoming instead a steel-industry engineer. Heir to the magnificent family collection—which comprises the largest single holding of Van Gogh works in existence—Mr. van Gogh in the 1960s turned the works over to a foundation and the Netherlands government agreed to build a new museum in Amsterdam to house them.

Vincent's work in Paris, and through Theo had asked for some pictures. Six were sent, including *The Red Vineyard,* the painting that was sold. The caliber of the exhibition may be gauged by the list of artists who participated, among them Redon, Lautrec, Renoir and Cézanne. The buyer of Vincent's painting was herself an artist, the Belgian Anna Bock. Although the price was only about $80, the quality of the show and of the buyer's taste was high; the sale seemed a good omen.

Most of the *Vingtistes* approved of Vincent's work or were diplomatically silent, but one member took exception. Henry de Groux, a painter of religious scenes, angrily refused to allow his pictures to be hung in the same hall with "the abominable *Pot of Sunflowers.*" At a banquet celebrating the opening of the exhibition, De Groux denounced the absent Van Gogh as "an ignoramus and a charlatan." This so offended Toulouse-Lautrec, a descendant of Crusaders, that he challenged De Groux to a duel. The encounter might have been a rousing one, as De Groux was scarcely taller than Lautrec and could have had difficulty coping with the furious "little blacksmith wearing pince-nez." However, the other artists intervened and no blood was shed. De Groux was permitted to resign from *Les Vingt* the next day.

The information about the sale of his painting, coming soon after the news of the magazine article, seems to have had a disastrous effect on Vincent in Saint-Rémy. Almost immediately he suffered another attack, from which he did not recover for several weeks. Then he wrote to his mother and a sister: "As soon as I heard that my work was having some success, and read the article in question, I feared at once that I should be punished for it; this is how things nearly always go in a painter's life: success is about the worst thing that can happen." His reaction to praise remained what it had been in his childhood, when he had torn up his drawing after his parents had spoken well of it.

After he had recovered enough to travel—on May 16, 1890—Vincent took an overnight train from southern France to Paris. He insisted on making the journey alone, to Theo's great concern, but arrived without incident. It was then that Theo's wife first saw him. "I had expected a sick man," she wrote, "but here was a sturdy, broad-shouldered man with a healthy color, a smile on his face and a very resolute appearance." Her impression was that Vincent was stronger than Theo, who suffered from a chronic kidney disease and was often unnerved by disputes with his maddeningly stodgy employers. She continued: "Then Theo drew him into the room where our little boy's cradle was. . . . Silently the two brothers looked at the quietly sleeping baby—both had tears in their eyes. Then Vincent turned smilingly to me and said, pointing to the simple crocheted cover on the cradle, 'Don't cover him with too much lace, little sister.'

"He stayed with us three days, and was cheerful and lively all the time. Saint-Rémy was not mentioned. He went out by himself to buy olives, which he used to eat every day and which he insisted on our eating too. The first morning he was up very early and was standing in his shirt sleeves looking at his pictures, of which our apartment was full. The walls were covered with them—in the dining room . . . *The Potato*

Eaters; in the sitting room the great *Landscape of Arles* and the *Night View on the Rhône.* Besides, to the great despair of our *femme de ménage,* there were under the bed, under the sofa, under the cupboards in the little spare room, huge piles of unframed canvases; they were now spread out on the floor and studied with great attention."

While Vincent was in Paris several of his friends, including Lautrec, Pissarro and Père Tanguy, came to visit him. The effort of talking to them fatigued him. He had thought that he might make some paintings in the city, but he became too agitated to work and was anxious to carry out the plan that Theo and Pissarro had made for him. Accordingly he departed for the village of Auvers-sur-Oise, about a half hour's journey northwest of Paris, taking with him a letter of introduction to the physician and friend of artists, Dr. Paul Gachet.

Vincent found Auvers "very beautiful, having among other things a lot of old thatched roofs . . . it is the real country, characteristic and picturesque." The village has changed but little since his time. The tree-shaded houses are scattered along a slope that ascends from the slow-moving Oise River; above them there is a vast plain of wheat fields, constantly patrolled by flocks of crows. A number of artists have been attracted by the quiet charm of Auvers, among them Daubigny, Guillaumin, Cézanne and Pissarro. Vincent found lodging for about 70 cents a day at a small inn—today the Café à Van Gogh—where on the third floor, under the eaves, a stifling cubbyhole is maintained in his memory. Dark, with one cloudy window high up on the slanting wall, it has barely space enough to contain a chest of drawers, a table and the narrow bed on which he is said to have died.

Dr. Gachet struck Vincent as "rather eccentric." Then in his sixties, the doctor had an abundance of red hair, a long, gloomy face and a fondness for controversial causes—among them socialism, free love and cremation. Another of his interests was a Society for Mutual Autopsy, into which he tried to recruit all his friends so that their hearts and brains could be studied after death. A widower, Gachet lived with his teen-age son and daughter in one of the largest houses in the village, surrounded by a half-dozen dogs and as many cats, rabbits, pigeons and ducks, as well as a goat, a tortoise and a peacock.

Following his initial reaction, Vincent became fond of the doctor, who repeatedly invited him to his house for dinner and reassured him about his illness—"He said to me besides that if the melancholy or anything else became too much for me to bear, he could easily do something to lessen its intensity. . . . Well, the moment when I need him may certainly come, however up to now all is well."

Informing Theo that Gachet was "very like you and me," Vincent sensed sadness and resignation beneath the eccentricity of the man and made a portrait of him *(page 175)* in which he caught "the heartbroken expression of our time." When he discovered a printing press in the doctor's house he produced the sole copperplate in all his work, an etched portrait of his host.

Drinking little, going to bed early and rising at five, Van Gogh worked in Auvers with almost as much zest as he had in Arles before his first attack. He painted the houses and gardens of the village, the flowering chestnut trees, the Gothic church and the great plain of wheat, turning out so many canvases (about 70 in 65 days) that it was impossible to store them in his little room. A Dutch painter, Anton Hirschig, who was also staying at the inn, recalled that Vincent piled his work "helter-skelter in the dirtiest little corner one can imagine, a sort of hovel where goats were usually kept. It was dark there, the walls were of brick without any plaster, with straw hanging from them. . . . And every day he brought new ones in; they were strewn on the floor and hanging on the walls. No one ever looked at them."

On a Sunday in June Theo and his family journeyed out from Paris for a picnic. "Vincent met us at the train," wrote Theo's wife, "and he brought a bird's nest as a plaything for his little nephew. . . . He insisted upon carrying the baby and had no rest until he had shown him all the animals in [Gachet's] yard. We lunched in the open air, and afterward took a long walk, the day was so peacefully quiet, so happy."

In the days following the visit Vincent's health continued to improve and he was optimistic. He thought again of exhibiting his work in a Paris café, and proposed to make a series of plates to be printed on Gachet's press. He even felt that he would be able to travel with Gauguin to Madagascar—if Gauguin should ask him. But for all his appearance of renewed well-being his life was very near its end.

Van Gogh did not kill himself during an attack of insanity; he seemed lucid to all who saw him in his last days. About a fortnight after the picnic in the country, Theo was obliged to send him disturbing news. The child had become deathly ill from drinking the "poisonous" milk sold in Paris. Theo and his wife were exhausted: "You never heard anything so grievously distressing as this almost continuous plaintive crying all through many days and many nights."

Theo also reported that his dispute with his employers, whom he now called "those rats," had reached such an impasse that he was thinking of resigning his job and attempting to establish himself as an independent dealer. This would involve risk; they might all have to live on reduced income. But he did his best to reassure his brother: "Don't bother your head about me or about us, old fellow, but remember that what gives me the greatest pleasure is the knowledge that you are in good health and busy with your work, which is admirable. You already have too much fire, and we must be in good shape to fight for a long time yet, for we shall have to battle all our lives rather than eat the oats of charity they give to old horses in the stables of the great. We shall draw the plow until our strength forsakes us, and we shall still look with admiration at the sun or the moon."

Vincent was not reassured; he went to Paris for a family conference that distressed him even more. Although the baby's health had improved, the three adults were unable to talk calmly. He returned to Auvers in a bleak mood and wrote a letter full of pessimism—"And the prospect grows darker, I see no happy future at all." He went to Dr. Gachet's house and quarreled with the well-meaning old man for no very good reason. Gachet had a painting by Armand Guillaumin which Vincent much admired, and for which the doctor had not yet bought a frame. Vincent thought the neglect was barbarous, and loudly upbraided Gachet. "I think we must not count on Dr. Gachet *at all*," he wrote Theo. "First of all, he is sicker than I am. . . . Now when one blind man leads another, don't they both fall into the ditch?" He implied that since Gachet was mad, further association with him might cause his own madness to return.

Theo's wife then tried her hand at a soothing letter, but to little effect. "It is no slight thing," replied Vincent, "when all of us feel our daily bread in danger; it is not a trifle when for other reasons also we feel that our existence is fragile. Back here, I still felt very sad and continued to feel the weight of the storm which threatens you. What can be done? You see, I generally try to be fairly cheerful, but my life too is menaced at its very root, and my steps also are wavering. I feared— not so much, but a little just the same—that being a burden to you, you felt me to be rather a thing to be dreaded." In the last sentence lay the heart of the matter: he feared, far more than "a little," that his dependence on Theo had become intolerable.

He resumed work, "though the brush almost slipped from my fingers." The subjects he chose were "vast fields of wheat under troubled skies, and I did not need to go out of my way to express sadness and extreme loneliness." In one of his three last paintings, *Wheat Field with Crows (pages 176-177)*, his anxiety is obvious. In an alarming inversion of perspective, the horizon appears to be rushing at the spectator as though to engulf him; nothing promises hope of escape.

On Sunday, July 27, 1890, he began a letter to Theo in which he repeated his long-held belief that "through me you have your part in the actual production of some canvases that will retain their calm even in the catastrophe. . . . Well, my own work, I am risking my life for it and my reason has half foundered because of it—that's all right . . . but what's the use?" He did not finish the letter, but apparently thrust it into his pocket and walked out of the inn toward the wheat fields. With him he carried a revolver, but he also carried his easel, perhaps not having made any decision as to when or even if he might shoot himself. It is not known where he obtained the gun; he may have borrowed it from one of the townsfolk, explaining that he wished to shoot at crows.

Vincent believed that life is endless. "At one time," he said, "the earth was supposed to be flat. Well, so it is, even today, from Paris to Asnières. But that fact doesn't prevent science from proving that the earth as a whole is spherical. No one nowadays denies it. Well . . . we are still at the stage of believing that life itself is flat, the distance from birth to death. Yet the probability is that life, too, is spherical and much more extensive and capacious than the hemisphere we know."

In another letter he wrote of "the eternal question whether we can see the whole of life or only know a hemisphere of it before death . . . the sight of stars always sets me dreaming just as naïvely as those black dots on a map set me dreaming of towns and villages. Why should these points of light in the firmament, I wonder, be less accessible than the dark ones on the map of France? We take a train to go to Tarascon or Rouen and we take death to go to a star. . . . Anyway, I don't see why cholera . . . or cancer should not be heavenly modes of loco-motion like ships, buses and trains here below, while if we die peacefully of old age we make the journey on foot."

He would not make the journey on foot, but neither would he make it with all possible speed. At a few hundred yards' distance from the inn he entered a farmyard, stepped behind a manure pile and shot him-self. He did not put the gun to his head or his heart but against his ab-domen. Then he walked back to the inn, falling repeatedly but still able to make his way up to his small, suffocating room.

The landlord discovered him there, lying on his bed with his face turned to the wall, and sent for help. Dr. Gachet thought it unwise to try to extract the bullet but told him that he might very well survive. "Then I will have to do it all over again," said Vincent. When Gachet asked for the address of Theo's home in Paris, Vincent refused to give it to him; it was necessary to send a message to his office. Theo did not re-ceive it until the next morning. In the interim the gendarmes of Auvers came to the inn, stood beside Vincent's bed and complained that he had committed a breach of the peace. He replied that his crime was his own affair. During the night he did not sleep, smoked his pipe and ut-tered not a word more.

When Theo arrived Vincent said, "Do not cry, I did it for the good of everybody." The brothers talked for most of the day, although Theo found time to send a note to his wife: "Poor fellow, fate has not given him much and he has no illusions left. Things are sometimes too hard, he feels so alone. . . . He inquired most urgently about you and the boy and said that he had not expected that life would bring him so many sor-rows. If only we could give him a little courage to live! Don't be too wor-ried; once before things looked desperate for him and yet his strong nature eventually cheated the doctors."

At 1 o'clock on Tuesday morning, nearly 36 hours after he had shot himself, Vincent said in Dutch, "I wish I could go home now," and died. His age was 37 years and four months.

The priest of Auvers denied a hearse to the suicide; it was necessary to borrow one from a neighboring village. A number of Vincent's friends came to Auvers for the funeral and one of them, the painter Émile Ber-nard, wrote of it: "On the walls of the room where his body lay all his last canvases were nailed, forming something like a halo around him and rendering—through the brilliance or genius which shone from them —his death even more deplorable for us artists. On the coffin a simple white drapery and masses of flowers, the sunflowers he loved so much, yellow dahlias, yellow flowers everywhere. It was his favorite color, if you remember, symbol of the light of which he dreamed in the hearts of men as well as in works of art. Near him also his easel, his folding stool and his brushes had been placed on the floor in front of the cof-fin. . . . At three o'clock the body was removed. His friends carried it to the hearse. Some of the people in the assembly wept. Theodore van Gogh, who adored his brother, who had always sustained him in his struggle for art and independence, sobbed pitifully without cease. . . .

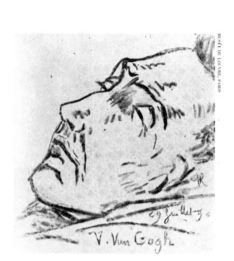

Sometime during the long day of July 29, 1890, while friends were arriving in Auvers for the funeral, Dr. Paul Gachet made a drawing of Van Gogh's body stretched out on the deathbed. The following afternoon Dr. Gachet was called upon to give a eulogy at the burial service, but the physician wept so much he could only stammer a few words. "He was an honest man," Gachet said, "and a great artist. He had only two aims: humanity and art. It was the art that he sought . . . which will insure his survival."

Outside, the sun was ferociously hot. We climbed the hill of Auvers talking of him, of the bold forward thrust he has given to art, of the great projects that always preoccupied him, of the good he has done to each of us. We arrived at the cemetery, a little new cemetery dotted with fresh tombstones. It is on a height overlooking the fields ready for reaping, under a wide blue sky he might still have loved—maybe. And then he was lowered into the grave. Who would not have cried at that moment —the day was too much to his liking to prevent us from thinking that he could still have lived happily."

Theo was shattered by grief; for weeks he could not even reply to the letters he received. When he recovered, his sole thought was to preserve Vincent's art and memory. He wrote to the young critic Albert Aurier suggesting that Aurier undertake a biography "for which I could furnish you all the material which is altogether authentic as I have had a very steady correspondence with him." Aurier was glad to accept the task but could not begin it immediately. Nor was he ever able to produce the biography. Two years later he died at 27 of typhoid fever.

Theo also attempted to stage an exhibition of Vincent's paintings. Apparently he did not even consider having it in his own gallery—his relations with his employers were far too strained for that. Instead he approached the great dealer Paul Durand-Ruel and asked for space. Durand-Ruel, who had earlier been driven to the verge of bankruptcy while supporting such unsalable artists as Monet and Renoir, perhaps did not now wish to risk promoting yet another. After Durand-Ruel's refusal Theo tried to set up the exhibition in the only place available: his own apartment. But he was overwhelmed by the problem of selecting the finest paintings from Vincent's enormous legacy. While he tried to cope with the task he had a last, violent quarrel with his employers, resigned from the firm and suddenly lost his mind.

At first his madness appeared mild. He became obsessed with carrying out projects that had been dear to Vincent and sent a telegram to Gauguin, who was painting in Brittany: "Departure to tropics assured, money follows—Theo, Director." He then attempted to rent the hall of Le Tambourin, the café where Vincent had hung his pictures three years earlier, and tried to revive the idea of a society of artists. Soon, however, he became violent and had to be locked up.

Within a short time Theo recovered sufficiently to be able to travel, and his wife took him to Holland. There he fell into a profound depression from which almost nothing could rouse him. His physician read him an article about Vincent in a Dutch paper, but only at the sound of his brother's name did he show a flicker of attention. He died on January 25, 1891, less than six months after Vincent. He was 33. As to the cause of his illness, the physician noted simply that Theo suffered from "overstrain and sorrow; he had a life full of emotional stress."

Theo was buried in Holland. Twenty-three years later his widow had his remains transferred to Auvers and placed beside Vincent's. The graves have a single cover of ivy. In the gentle seasons of the year strangers come to drop yellow flowers there; one scarcely fades before another falls beside it.

Last Rush of Genius

The sporadic fits of illness and despair that finally drove Van Gogh to suicide altered neither the quality nor the quantity of his art. Even after the incident at Arles, when he sliced off part of an ear, Van Gogh worked himself mercilessly, his painting interrupted only temporarily. As the fury of each attack passed, he became as lucid as ever, painting landscapes, portraits, self-portraits *(right)* and writing scores of clear, logical letters. Although he was distraught about his lapses, he knew they had not ruined his art; he wrote Theo, "You will see that the canvases I have done in the intervals are steady and not inferior to the others."

Ill and alone, Van Gogh found refuge in work. He painted prolifically during the year he spent in an asylum at Saint-Rémy, near Arles. Returning north in May 1890, he visited Theo, his wife and their newly born son, Vincent, in Paris. He then settled in Auvers-sur-Oise, a little town some 20 miles northwest of Paris, where he expended his last burst of creative energy. Pushing himself to exhaustion, Van Gogh completed some 60 paintings in two months; in the last year and a half of his life, from his first severe attack of mental illness to his suicide, his output was prodigious, totaling some 300 paintings and several hundred drawings. Nor was his work that of a madman. His mature style, which flourished at Arles, became even freer; his last paintings are brilliant in color, fluid in line and pungently expressive.

Van Gogh's artistic strength and lucidity are evident in this self-portrait, done while he was recuperating from his self-mutilation in Arles. The eyes are piercing, their blue cast heightened by the blood-red horizon placed exactly at their level. Above all, this portrait shows Van Gogh's incredible artistic detachment; no matter how painful it might have been, he was able to see himself as he was—a haunted, driven man.

Self-Portrait with Pipe and Bandaged Ear, Arles, February 1889

169

Road with Cypress and Stars, Saint-Rémy, May 1890

The Plain Near Auvers, July 1890

During his stay at the asylum at Saint-Rémy, Van Gogh often spent his days roaming the nearby countryside painting landscapes. One of the last pictures he did there, *Road with Cypress and Stars (left)*, reveals the style that he had evolved: swirling brush strokes, thick impasto, dynamic composition. Van Gogh, fond of this work as a remembrance of the south, described it in a letter to Gauguin: "I still have a cypress with a star from down there, a last attempt—a night sky with a moon without brilliance, the slender crescent barely emerging from the opaque shadow cast by the earth— a star with an exaggerated radiance, if you like, a soft brilliance of pink and green in the ultramarine sky, where some clouds are hurrying. Below, a road bordered with tall yellow canes, behind these the blue Lower Alps, an old inn with orange lighted windows, and a very tall cypress, very straight, very somber."

Van Gogh continued to prove his mastery of landscapes when he went north to Auvers. The painting above displays a vast panorama, the tall grass in the foreground emphasized by long slashes of paint, the fields, trees and clouds in the distance sharply defined. Even working quickly, he was still the careful craftsman, as the extraordinary detail on the following pages shows.

The Church at Auvers, June 1890

At Auvers Van Gogh worked furiously to distract his mind from its torments. During this period, he painted the Gothic church at Auvers *(above)*, an electric study with a cobalt-blue sky and acid-green grass.

One of Van Gogh's few friends at Auvers was Dr. Gachet, a physician who encouraged the artist to continue his work. Dr. Gachet's kindly nature appealed to Van Gogh but his eccentricity startled him. As Vincent wrote Theo, "He certainly appears to me just as ill and confused as you or I." A friend of the painters Pissarro and Cézanne, Dr. Gachet eagerly sat for a portrait by Van Gogh. Of the result *(above, right)*,

Portrait of Dr. Gachet, Auvers, June 1890

Vincent said, "Now I have a portrait of Dr. Gachet with the heartbroken expression of our time."

Indeed, Van Gogh saw much in the wan, vulnerable physician that reminded him of himself and his own suffering. He painted the man resting resignedly on an elbow; the books of an intellectual lie on the table, and in the glass before him is a sprig of foxglove, a medicinal herb. But the focus of the painting is the doctor's sensitive face. His ultramarine coat, seen against a background of hills painted in a lighter blue, sets off the tired, pale features and transparent blue eyes that reflect the compassion and the melancholy of the man.

175

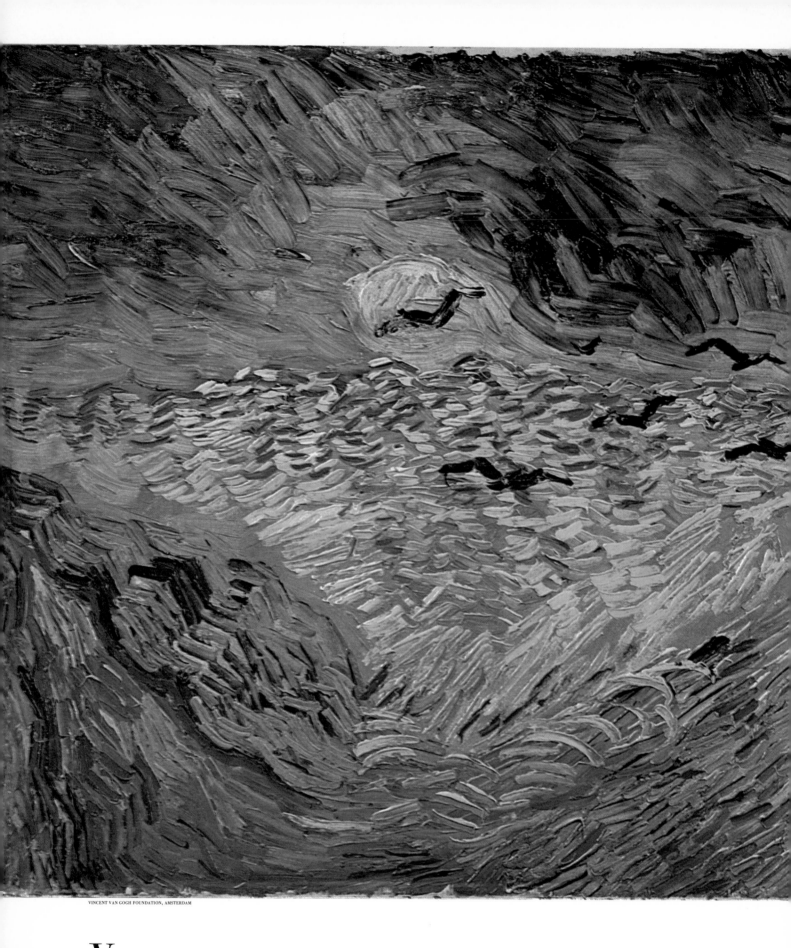

Vincent wrote Theo that he had found no difficulty in expressing "sadness and extreme loneliness" in the last three paintings he created, one of which is shown above. Signs of his grief—and his fears—abound in this turbulently emotional work. The sky is a deep, angry blue that overpowers the two clouds on the horizon. The foreground is uncertain—an ill-defined crossroad. A dirt path seen in part in the foreground runs blindly off both sides of the canvas; a grass track curves into the wheat field only to disappear at a dead end. The wheat itself

176

Wheat Field with Crows, Auvers, July 1890

rises like an angry sea to contend with the stormy sky. Crows flapping over the tumult swarm toward the viewer. Even the perspective contributes to this effect; the horizon rolls relentlessly forward. In this picture Van Gogh painted what he must have felt—that the world was closing in on him and his roads of escape were blocked, with the land rising up and the sky glowering down. Created in the artist's deepest anxiety, the painting nevertheless reveals Van Gogh's power, his expressive use of color and firm sense of composition.

177

(1) Antwerp, November 1885-February 1886

(2) Paris, 1887

(5) Paris, January-February 1888

(6) Arles, September 1888

No more fitting epilogue can be provided for Van Gogh than this series of self-portraits, which reveal the changes in his style and his growing self-awareness. An early study (1) shows the Dutch influence of dark, earthy tones. His palette grew lighter and more intense in Paris (2, 3, 4, 5). The hues of Arles reminded Van Gogh of

178

(3) Paris, 1887

(4) Paris, September-December 1887

(7) Saint-Rémy or Auvers, 1889-1890

(8) Saint-Rémy or Auvers, late 1889-1890

Japanese prints and he painted himself as a Buddhist monk (6). After his mental breakdown, he saw himself as an apparition emerging from an ambiguous background (7). His last self-portrait (8, and detail on the following page) is a powerful study of a fevered mind held in check by a monumental effort of will.

Van Gogh's ruthless honesty pours forth from his final self-portrait, completed some months before his suicide. Tormented by recurring moments of insanity, the artist resolutely viewed himself and painted a tortured soul battling desperately against the terrors that surrounded him. His face is stoically set, his lips firm, his eyes hypnotic in their determination.

The shock waves caused by the loss of Vincent were disastrous; they shattered the health of his brother Theo, destroying his sanity as well. Within six months he too was dead. The extent of Theo's despair is revealed in a letter he wrote his mother soon after Vincent's death: "One cannot write how grieved one is nor find any comfort. It is a grief that will last and which I certainly shall never forget as long as I live; the only thing one might say is that he himself has the rest he was longing for. . . . Life was such a burden to him; but now, as often happens, everybody is full of praise for his talents. . . . Oh Mother! He was so my own, own brother."

Chronology: Artists of Van Gogh's Era

1800 1875 1950

HOLLAND
JOHANN JONGKIND 1819-1891
JOSEF ISRAËLS 1824-1911
JACOB MARIS 1837-1899
ANTON MAUVE 1838-1888
MATTHEW MARIS 1839-1917
WILLEM MARIS 1844-1910
VINCENT VAN GOGH 1853-1890
GEORGE HENDRIK BREITNER 1857-1923
PIET MONDRIAN 1872-1944
KEES VAN DONGEN 1877-1968

SPAIN
PABLO PICASSO 1881-
JUAN GRIS 1887-1927

FRANCE
JEAN-BAPTISTE CAMILLE COROT 1796-1875
EUGÈNE DELACROIX 1798-1863
HONORÉ DAUMIER 1808-1879
THÉODORE ROUSSEAU 1812-1867
JEAN-FRANÇOIS MILLET 1814-1875
CHARLES FRANÇOIS DAUBIGNY 1817-1878
GUSTAVE COURBET 1819-1877
ADOLPHE MONTICELLI 1824-1886
PIERRE PUVIS DE CHAVANNES 1824-1898
WILLIAM ADOLPHE BOUGUEREAU 1825-1905
GUSTAVE MOREAU 1826-1898
JULES BRETON 1827-1906
CAMILLE PISSARRO 1830-1903
PAUL GUSTAVE DORÉ 1832-1883
ÉDOUARD MANET 1832-1883
EDGAR DEGAS 1834-1917
JULES CHÉRET 1836-1932
PAUL CÉZANNE 1839-1906
ALFRED SISLEY 1839-1899
ODILON REDON 1840-1916
AUGUSTE RODIN 1840-1917
CLAUDE MONET 1840-1926
BERTHE MORISOT 1841-1895
JEAN BAPTISTE GUILLAUMIN 1841-1927
PIERRE-AUGUSTE RENOIR 1841-1919
HENRI ROUSSEAU 1844-1903
PAUL GAUGUIN 1848-1903
GEORGES SEURAT 1859-1891
ARISTIDE MAILLOL 1861-1944
PAUL SIGNAC 1863-1935
HENRI DE TOULOUSE-LAUTREC 1864-1901
HENRI MATISSE 1869-1954
MAURICE DENIS 1870-1943
GEORGES ROUAULT 1871-1958
ALBERT MARQUET 1875-1947

1800 1875 1950

GERMANY
HANS VON MARÉES 1837-1887
MAX LIEBERMANN 1847-1935
LOVIS CORINTH 1858-1925
EMIL NOLDE 1867-1956
LYONEL FEININGER 1871-1956
FRANZ MARC 1880-1916

SWITZERLAND
ARNOLD BOECKLIN 1827-1901
FERDINAND HODLER 1853-1918
PAUL KLEE 1879-1940

ITALY
CARLO CARRÀ 1881-1966
UMBERTO BOCCIONI 1882-1916
GINO SEVERINI 1883-1966
AMEDEO MODIGLIANI 1884-1920
GIORGIO DI CHIRICO 1888-

ENGLAND
WILLIAM HUNT 1827-1910
DANTE ROSSETTI 1828-1882
JOHN MILLAIS 1829-1896
EDWARD BURNE-JONES 1833-1898

AUSTRIA
GUSTAV KLIMT 1862-1918
OSKAR KOKOSCHKA 1886-
EGON SCHIELE 1890-1918

SCANDINAVIA
EDVARD MUNCH 1863-1944

EASTERN EUROPE AND RUSSIA
ALEXEI VON JAWLENSKY 1864-1941
WASSILY KANDINSKY 1866-1944
FRANK KUPKA 1871-1957
CONSTANTIN BRANCUSI 1876-1957
CASIMIR MALEVICH 1878-1935
MARC CHAGALL 1887-

UNITED STATES
GEORGE INNESS 1825-1894
ALBERT BIERSTADT 1830-1902
JAMES McNEILL WHISTLER 1834-1903
WINSLOW HOMER 1836-1910
THOMAS EAKINS 1844-1916
MARY CASSATT 1845-1926
ALBERT RYDER 1847-1917
WILLIAM HARNETT 1848-1892
JOHN SINGER SARGENT 1856-1925
CHILDE HASSAM 1859-1935
MAURICE PRENDERGAST 1861-1924
ROBERT HENRI 1865-1929
JOHN MARIN 1870-1953

1800 1875 1950

Van Gogh's predecessors, contemporaries and successors are grouped chronologically by country. The bands correspond to the artists' life spans.

Bibliography

VAN GOGH—HIS LIFE AND WORK

Auden, W. H. (editor), *Van Gogh, A Self-Portrait.** E. P. Dutton & Co., Inc., 1963.

Cabanne, Pierre, *Van Gogh.* Translated by Mary I. Martin. Prentice-Hall, Inc., 1963.

The Complete Letters of Vincent van Gogh, 3 vols., 2nd ed. New York Graphic Society, 1959.

Cooper, Douglas, *Van Gogh Drawings and Watercolors.* Macmillan & Co., 1955.

de la Faille, J. B.:
L'Oeuvre de Vincent van Gogh. Catalogue raisonné, 4 vols. Les Éditions G. van Oest, Paris and Brussels, 1928.
Vincent van Gogh. Translated by Prudence Montagu-Pollock. French and European Publications, 1939.

Elgar, Frank, *Van Gogh.** Translated by James Cleugh. Frederick A. Praeger, 1958.

Erpel, Fritz, *Van Gogh Self-Portraits.* Translated by Doris Edwards. Bruno Cassirer, 1964.

Estienne, Charles, *Van Gogh.* Translated by S. J. C. Harrison. Taste of Our Time Series. Albert Skira, Lausanne, 1953.

Graetz, H. R., *The Symbolic Language of Vincent van Gogh.* McGraw-Hill, 1963.

Hammacher, A. M., *Genius and Disaster: The Ten Creative Years of Vincent van Gogh.* Harry N. Abrams, Inc., 1968.

Leymarie, Jean, *Qui Était Van Gogh?* Albert Skira, 1968.

Nagera, Humberto, *Vincent van Gogh: A Psychological Study.* International Universities Press, 1967.

Nordenfalk, Carl, *The Life and Work of Van Gogh.* Philosophical Library, 1953.

Roskill, Mark (editor), *The Letters of Vincent van Gogh.* Zontana Library, Atheneum Publishers, 1963.

Schapiro, Meyer, *Vincent van Gogh.* The Library of Great Painters. Harry N. Abrams, 1950.

Tralbaut, Mark Edo:
Van Gogh: A Pictorial Biography. The Viking Press, 1959.
Van Gogh te Antwerpen. Outwikkeling, 1958.
Vincent van Gogh in Drenthe. De Torenlaan, 1959.
Vincent van Gogh in Zijn Antwerpsche Periode. A.J.G., Strengholt, 1948.

Vanbeselaere, Walther, *De Hollandsche Periode in Het Werk van Vincent van Gogh.* De Sikkel, 1937.

Vincent van Gogh. A Choice of Paintings and Drawings from the Collection of the Vincent van Gogh Foundation. Stedelijk Museum, Amsterdam, 1968.

Vincent van Gogh Catalogue. Rijksmuseum Kröller-Müller, Otterlo, 1966.

ART—HISTORICAL BACKGROUND

Goldwater, Robert J., *Primitivism in Modern Art,** rev. ed. Vintage Books, 1967.

Hamilton, George Heard, *Painting and Sculpture in Europe, 1880-1940.* Penguin, 1967.

Rewald, John:
The History of Impressionism. The Museum of Modern Art, 1961.
Post-Impressionism: From Van Gogh to Gauguin. The Museum of Modern Art, 1956.

PAUL GAUGUIN

Bodelsen, Merete, *Gauguin's Ceramics.* Faber and Faber, London, 1964.

Danielsson, Bengt, *Gauguin in the South Seas.* Translated by Reginald Spink. Doubleday, 1966.

Gauguin: Paintings, Drawings, Prints, Sculpture. The Art Institute of Chicago, 1959.

Goldwater, Robert, *Paul Gauguin.* The Library of Great Painters. Harry N. Abrams.

Gray, Christopher, *Sculpture and Ceramics of Paul Gauguin.* The Johns Hopkins Press, 1963.

Huyghe, René, *Gauguin.* Translated by Helen C. Slonim. Crown Publishers, Inc., 1959.

Leymarie, Jean (editor), *Paul Gauguin: Water-Colours, Pastels and Drawings in Colour.* Faber and Faber, London, 1961.

Paul Gauguin's Intimate Journals. Translated by Van Wyck Brooks. Indiana University Press, 1965.

Perruchot, Henri, *Gauguin.* Translated by Humphrey Hare. Perpetua Books, London, 1963.

HENRI DE TOULOUSE-LAUTREC

Adhémar, Jean (editor), *Toulouse-Lautrec, His Complete Lithographs and Drypoints.* Harry N. Abrams, Inc., 1965.

Bouret, Jean, *The Life and Work of Toulouse-Lautrec.* Translated by Daphne Woodward. Harry N. Abrams, Inc., 1966.

Cooper, Douglas (editor), *Toulouse-Lautrec.* Harry N. Abrams, Inc., 1956.

Dortu, M. G., and Ph. Huisman, *Lautrec by Lautrec.* Translated by Corinne Bellow. The Viking Press, 1964.

Jourdain, Francis, and Jean Adhémar, *Toulouse-Lautrec.* Pierre Tisné, 1952.

Perruchot, Henri, *Toulouse-Lautrec.* Translated by Humphrey Hare. Perpetua Books, London, 1960.

Acknowledgments

For their help in the production of this book the author and editors wish to thank the following people and institutions: Wilhelm F. Arntz, Director, Art Archive, Haab/Upper Bavaria; Countess Mary Attems, Naucelle, Aveyron; Cynthia Carter, Photograph and Slide Library, and Harriet Cooper, Public Relations Department, The Metropolitan Museum of Art, New York; C. N. J. De Groot, Secretary, Rijksmuseum Kröller-Müller, Otterlo; Enno Develing, Conservator, Hague Municipal Museum, The Hague; Jean Devoisins, Administrateur Délégué du Musée Toulouse-Lautrec, Albi; P. A. Frequin, Administrator, Hague Municipal Museum, The Hague; Mme. Guynet-Pechadre, Conservateur, Service Photographique, Musée du Louvre, Paris; Deane Hancock, Museum of Fine Arts, Boston; P. C. Le Grand, Oegstgeest; E. R. Meyer, Director, Vincent van Gogh Foundation, Amsterdam; Municipal Register, Dordrecht; Municipal and State Archives, Haarlem; Nederlandse Bank, Amsterdam; Reproduction and Photo Department, Stedelijk Museum, Amsterdam; Jean-Marie Roghi, Secrétaire Général Adjoint, Mairie d'Arles, Arles; Jean-Maurice Rouquette, Conservateur des Musées d'Arles, Arles; G. J. Nieuwenhuizen Segaar, The Hague; Richard L. Tooke, The Museum of Modern Art, New York; Germaine Tureau, Chief, Section Commerciale de la Photothèque des Musées Nationaux, Paris; V. W. van Gogh, President, Vincent van Gogh Foundation, Laren; Van Gogh Department, State Bureau for Art Historical Documentation, The Hague; Vincent van Gogh Foundation, Amsterdam.

The quotations on pages 97, 98 and 99 were reprinted from *Paul Gauguin's Intimate Journals*, translated by Van Wyck Brooks, with the permission of Liveright, Publishers, New York, copyright © 1955, Liveright Publishing Corporation.

Fishing Boats on the Beach at Saintes-Maries, June 1888. A detail of Van Gogh's painting appears in color on the slipcase.

Picture Credits

Index

Numerals in italics indicate a picture of the subject mentioned. Unless otherwise specified, all listed art works are by Van Gogh. Dimensions are given in inches; height precedes width.

The text for this book was photocomposed in Bodoni Book, a typeface named for its Italian designer, Giambattista Bodoni (1740-1813). One of the earliest modern typefaces, Bodoni Book differs from more evenly weighted old-style characters in the greater contrast between thick and thin parts of letters. The Bodoni character is vertical with a thin, straight serif.

XXXXXXX

PRINTED IN U.S.A.